ANTHOLOGY FOR

The Musician's Guide
to Theory and Analysis

THIRD EDITION

ANTHOLOGY FOR

The Musician's Guide
to Theory and Analysis

THIRD EDITION

Jane Piper Clendinning
Florida State University College of Music

Elizabeth West Marvin
Eastman School of Music

W. W. NORTON & COMPANY
NEW YORK · LONDON

W. W. Norton & Company has been independent since its founding in 1923, when William Warder Norton and Mary D. Herter Norton first published lectures delivered at the People's Institute, the adult education division of New York City's Cooper Union. The Nortons soon expanded their program beyond the Institute, publishing books by celebrated academics from America and abroad. By mid-century, the two major pillars of Norton's publishing program—trade books and college texts—were firmly established. In the 1950s, the Norton family transferred control of the company to its employees, and today—with a staff of four hundred and a comparable number of trade, college, and professional titles published each year—W. W. Norton & Company stands as the largest and oldest publishing house owned wholly by its employees.

Editor: Justin Hoffman
Editorial Assistant: Grant Phelps
Managing editor, College: Marian Johnson
Associate Project Editor: Michael Fauver
Media Editor: Steve Hoge
Media Editorial Assistant: Stephanie Eads
Production Manager: Jane Searle
Design Director: Rubina Yeh
Designers: Rubina Yeh and David Botwinik
Composition and layout: Code Mantra
Manufacturing by Transcontinental

ISBN: 978-0-393-28319-8

W. W. Norton & Company, Inc., 500 Fifth Avenue, New York, NY 10110
www.wwnorton.com
W. W. Norton & Company, Ltd., Castle House, 75/76 Wells Street, London WIT3QT

5 6 7 8 9 0

Contents

Preface

The study of music theory is at its very heart an aural endeavor: its study is all about sounds—how and why music sounds the way it does. For this reason, we strongly believe in approaching theoretical instruction aurally, by listening repeatedly to diverse pieces of music and drawing out their structural principles through that experience. This anthology is designed to accompany our textbook, *The Musician's Guide to Theory and Analysis*, but it can easily be adapted for use with any number of music theory texts that cover harmony, counterpoint, and form in tonal and post-tonal music. Our text's approach to learning music theory is a spiral one, in which we revisit the anthology's core repertoire from chapter to chapter as we introduce new concepts. A single piece might be used first to illustrate scales, then be revisited to study its triads, cadence types, secondary dominants, common-chord modulation, sequence, and binary form. We hope that by listening to these works often you will get to know the compositions in the anthology well—until you can hear each one in your head, the same way you can hear familiar songs just by thinking about them.

Why use an anthology in an era of free public-domain scores? By providing a collection of carefully selected scores—all coordinating with the textbook—we've saved you time and effort. Recordings of every work in the anthology—now online and included free with every new copy of the *Musician's Guide to Theory and Analysis*—make this anthology exceptionally useful and an outstanding value. We have taken considerable care in choosing music that we like, that many of our students have performed, and that they (and we) have enjoyed exploring together. We've selected works for a wide range of instruments and representing a number of genres, so that the music will be engaging for everyone. Some of the works should be familiar to you (Bach inventions, Gershwin's "I Got Rhythm," Sousa's "The Stars and Stripes Forever," Beethoven's *Für Elise*, and the hymn "A Mighty Fortress"), while others will probably be new. Some are classics of the repertoire: Mozart and Beethoven piano sonata movements, German lieder from Schubert and Schumann song cycles, and groundbreaking compositions by Penderecki and Reich.

In the third edition, we have worked to incorporate the ideas of helpful reviewers while retaining the key features that students and professors have appreciated about the first and second editions. The anthology features over 100 works, including:

- 31 twentieth-century compositions
- Arias and art songs (with translations to help analyze text painting)
- Music by women and African-American composers
- Music in popular genres, including ragtime and Broadway songs
- Music for band, wind ensemble, string quartet, and orchestra
- Music for choir, including anthems, hymns, and chorales
- Music featuring a range of solo instruments
- Keyboard works for piano, fortepiano, harpsichord, and organ

In response to feedback from reviewers, this edition includes twenty-three new works, including compositions by Alban Berg, Claude Debussy, John Cage, Elisabeth-Claude Jacquet de la Guerre, Stephen Foster, Gustav Holst, Jerome Kern, Maurice Ravel, and Clara Schumann.

Our Thanks to ...

A work of this size and scope is helped along the way by many people. We are especially grateful for the support of our families—Elizabeth A. Clendinning, David Stifler, Rachel Armstrong Bowers, and Rocky Bowers; and Glenn, Russell, and Caroline West. Our work together as co-authors has been incredibly rewarding, and we are thankful for that collaboration and friendship. We also thank Joel Phillips (Westminster Choir College) for his many important contributions—pedagogical, musical, and personal—to our project, and especially for the coordinated aural skills component of this package, *The Musician's Guide to Aural Skills* with Paul Murphy (Muhlenberg College), who has become a key member of our team. Thanks especially to Tim Pack (University of Oregon) for creating the Index of Teaching Points that now appears in this volume. While working on the project, we have received encouragement and useful ideas from our students at Florida State University and the Eastman School of Music, as well as from music theory teachers across the country. We thank these teachers for their willingness to share their years of experience with us.

For subvention of the recordings that accompany the text and anthology, and for his continued support of strong music theory pedagogy, we thank Jamal Rossi (Dean of the Eastman School of Music). For production of all recordings, our thanks go to recording engineers Mike Farrington and John Ebert, who worked tirelessly with Elizabeth Marvin on recording and editing sessions, as well as to Helen Smith, who oversees Eastman's Office of Technology and Media Production. We also acknowledge the strong contributions of David Peter Coppen, archivist of the Eastman Audio Archive, for his work contacting faculty and alumni for permission to include their performances among our recordings. We finally thank the faculty and students of the Eastman School who gave so generously of their time to make these recordings. The joy of their music making contributed mightily to this project.

We are indebted to the W. W. Norton staff for their commitment to *The Musician's Guide* series and their painstaking care in producing these volumes. Most notable among these are Justin Hoffman, who steered the entire effort with a steady hand and enthusiastic support; Susan Gaustad, whose knowledge of music and detailed, thoughtful questions made her a joy to work with; and Maribeth Payne, whose vision helped launch the series. Michael Fauver project edited the anthology, and Debra Nichols provided expert proofreading. Megan Jackson pursued copyright permissions and helped us understand relevant aspects of copyright law. Our gratitude to one and all.

Jane Piper Clendinning
Elizabeth West Marvin

ANTHOLOGY FOR

The Musician's Guide
to Theory and Analysis

THIRD EDITION

Anonymous
Minuet in D Minor, from the *Anna Magdalena Bach Notebook*

This minuet, by an unknown composer, is part of a collection of short keyboard compositions by Johann Sebastian Bach and others. The collection appears in a notebook that Bach gave to his second wife, Anna Magdalena, in 1725. In the early eighteenth century, such notebooks were useful tools for teaching performance and composition, and Bach assembled several for his family.

Anonymous
"The Ash Grove"

"The Ash Grove" is a traditional Welsh folk song that has been sung to various lyrics. The words shown here are by the nineteenth-century English playwright John Oxenford. Two versions follow: a lead sheet, in which the performer improvises an accompaniment from chord symbols, and an arrangement for piano.

Lead sheet

Arrangement by Joel Phillips

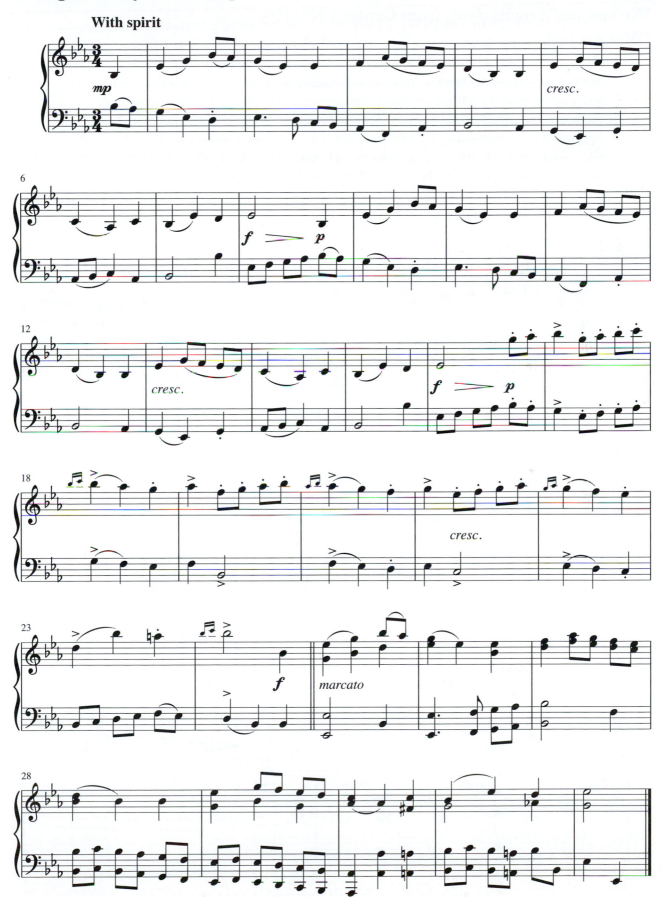

Johann Sebastian Bach (1685–1750)
"Er kommt" (recitative), from Cantata No. 140,
"Wachet auf"

Most of Bach's cantatas were written for performance in Lutheran church services, with texts expounding upon the religious themes of the particular day for which they were written. Cantatas frequently include polyphonic choral movements, arias for soloists, and chorale settings. While composition dates for most Bach cantatas are not known, we know this one was composed in 1731 for the Thomaskirche in Leipzig, where Bach served as Kappellmeister (music director), because it relates to the Parable of the Ten Virgins, which appears in the liturgical calendar on the twenty-seventh Sunday after Trinity—a date that only occurs when Easter is very early. The keyboard part shown is a modern realization of the figured bass.

No. 2. Recitative

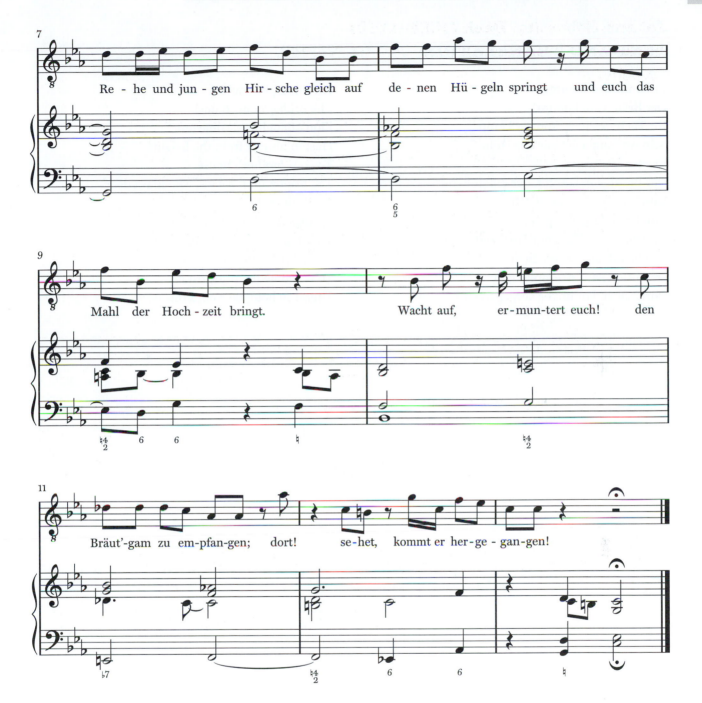

TEXT AND TRANSLATION

Er kommt, er kommt,	He comes, he comes,
Der Bräut'gam kommt!	The bridegroom comes!
Ihr Töchter Zions, kommt heraus,	Zion's daughters, come out,
Sein Ausgang eilet aus der Höhe	Hasten his exit from the heights
In euer Mutter Haus.	To your mother's house.
Der Bräut'gam kommt, der einen Rehe	The bridegroom comes, who like a deer
Und jungen Hirsche gleich	And young stag
Auf denen Hügeln springt	Springs from the hills,
Und euch das Mahl der Hochzeit bringt.	To bring you the wedding feast.
Wacht auf, ermuntert euch!	Wake up, be encouraged
Den Bräut'gam zu empfangen;	To welcome the bridegroom.
Dort! sehet, kommt er hergegangen!	There! Behold, he comes this way!

Johann Sebastian Bach
"Soll denn der Pales Opfer" (recitative)
and "Schafe können sicher weiden" (aria),
from Cantata No. 208 (*The Hunt*)

Bach's Hunt Cantata, a secular work, was first performed in 1713 for the birthday of Prince
Christian of Saxon-Weißenfels. The libretto, which borrows from Greek mythology, was written
by the German poet Salomo Franck, whose texts appear in dozens of Bach's cantatas. Although
the cantata as a whole is not frequently performed today, this aria has become well known on its
own, and its imagery of the shepherd watching over the flock has been adapted from its secular
origins to sacred uses. The keyboard part shown is a modern realization of the continuo bass,
for which very few figures were provided.

Libretto by Salomo Franck

wo - ein_ gu - ter Hir - te__ wacht, Scha - fe_ kön - nen si - cher_ wei - den,_

Scha - fe__ kön - nen si - cher__ wei - den,_ wo - ein gu - ter_

Hir - te wacht, wo - ein_ gu - ter Hir - te__

Wo Re - gen - ten wohl re - gie - ren, __ kann man __

Ruh' und Frie - den __ spü - ren, __ Ruh' _____ und __ Frie -

TEXT AND TRANSLATION

Soll denn der Pales Opfer hier das letzte sein? Nein!
  Nein!

Ich will die Pflicht auch niederlegen,
Und da das ganze Land vom Vivat schallt,
Auch dieses schöne Feld
Zu Ehren unserm Sachsenheld
Zur Freud' und Lust bewegen!

Schafe können sicher weiden,
Wo ein guter Hirte wacht.
Wo Regenten wohl regieren,
Kann man Ruh' und Friede spüren
Und was Länder glücklich macht.

So, shall Pales' offering here be the last? No, no!

I want also to set aside my duty,
And since the whole land with "Vivat" * echoes—
Even this beautiful field—
To honor our Saxon hero,
To stir to joy and passion.

Sheep may safely graze
Where a good shepherd keeps watch.
Where rulers rule well,
One can feel peace and tranquility,
And that which makes countries fortunate.

* Latin: May he live!

Johann Sebastian Bach
Chaconne, from Violin Partita No. 2 in D Minor

In 1720, Bach completed a set of six compositions for unaccompanied violin, including three partitas (or suites of dance movements). This Chaconne, which concludes the second partita, is longer than the rest of the composition's movements put together. While posing significant challenges for violinists, it remains a remarkable example of a polyphonic form set for a solo instrument.

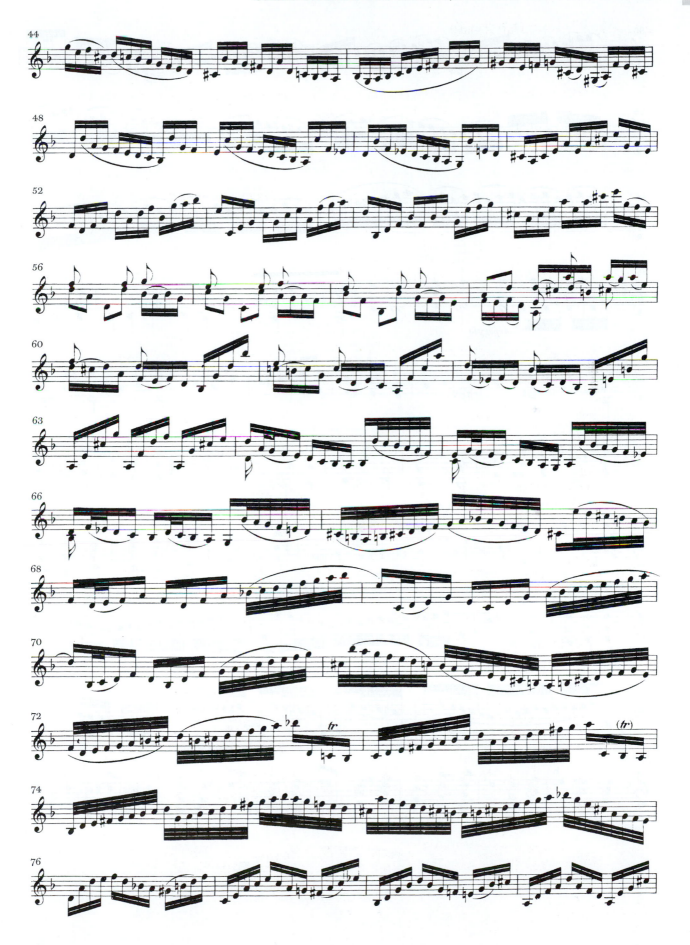

Johann Sebastian Bach
Chorales
"Aus meines Herzens Grunde" (No. 1)

The German Lutheran chorale tradition featured congregational singing of familiar melodies that were harmonized by many composers of the era. These tunes were well known to audiences of the time, and were also featured in variation sets, organ chorale preludes, and as movements of larger choral works. "Aus meines Herzens Grunde" is the first chorale in the collection of 317 of J. S. Bach's chorale harmonizations edited by his son, C. P. E. Bach, first published in four volumes between 1784 and 1787.

TEXT AND TRANSLATION

Aus meines Herzens Grunde
Sag' ich dir Lob und Dank,
In dieser Morgenstunde
Darzu mein Lebelang,
O Gott in deinem Thron,
Dir zu Lob, Preis und Ehren,
Durch Christum, unsern Herren,
Dein' eingebornen Sohn.

From my heart's foundation
I offer you praise and thanks,
In this morning hour,
Through my whole life long.
O God on your throne,
To you praise, exaltation, and honor,
Through Christ, our Lord,
Your only begotten son.

"Ein feste Burg ist unser Gott" (No. 20)

Both the words and melody to "Ein feste Burg ist unser Gott" (A Mighty Fortress Is Our God) were written by Martin Luther between 1527 and 1529. Luther, originally a Catholic priest, touched off the Protestant Reformation in Germany with his *Ninety-Five Theses*, which disputed a number of practices of the Catholic Church, particularly the sale of indulgences (documents granting forgiveness of sins). This hymn quickly became an anthem of the reform movement. Luther's melody is harmonized here by J. S. Bach. Many of Bach's chorales harmonize previously written melodies.

TEXT AND TRANSLATION

Ein feste Burg ist unser Gott,
ein gute Wehr und Waffen;
er hilft uns frei aus aller Not,
die uns itzt hat betroffen.
Der alte böse Feind,
mit Ernst er's jetzt meint,
groß Macht und viel List
sein grausam Rüstung ist,
auf Erd ist nicht sein gleichen.

A mighty fortress is our God,
A good defense and weapon;
He helps free us from all troubles
That now have struck us.
The old evil foe
With earnestness now intends
Great power and deceit.
His armor is cruel,
On earth is not his equal.

"O Haupt voll Blut und Wunden" (No. 74)

This chorale appears repeatedly in the *St. Matthew Passion,* a musical retelling of the story of the crucifixion, each time with a different text and harmonization. Bach composed the passion in 1727 for performance in the Thomaskirche. This chorale, in one of Bach's harmonizations, is still sung in Protestant churches today in the season of Lent, preceding Easter.

O Haupt voll Blut und Wun - den, voll Schmerz und vol - ler Hohn,
o Haupt, zu Spott ge - bun - den mit ei - ner Dor - nen - kron,

o Haupt, sonst schön ge - zie - ret mit höch - ster Ehr und Zier, jetzt

a - ber hoch schimp - fie - ret, ge - grü - ßet seist du mir!

TEXT AND TRANSLATION

O Haupt voll Blut und Wunden	O head, full of blood and wounds,
Voll Schmerz und voller Hohn,	Full of sorrow and full of scorn,
O Haupt, zu Spott gebunden	O head, to mockery bound
Mit einer Dornenkron,	With a crown of thorns,
O Haupt, sonst schön gezieret	O head, once beautifully adorned
Mit höchster Ehr und Zier	With highest honor and renown,
Jetzt aber hoch schimpfieret,	But now highly insulted,
Gegrüsset seist du mir!	Let me salute you!

"Wachet auf" (No. 179)

The chorale melody "Wachet auf" appears in several movements of Bach's Cantata No. 140 (1731) of the same name: as the theme for a polyphonic choral movement, as the cantus firmus for a ritornello-based movement, and as a four-part chorale. This harmonization is the last movement of the cantata. Another movement from this cantata is the recitative "Er kommt" (p. 4), and the chorale prelude (p. 29) is a transcription for organ of the ritornello-based movement.

Wohl - auf, der Bräut' - gam kommt,

Steht auf, die Lamp - en nehmt!

Hal - le - lu - jah! Macht

euch be - reit zu der Hoch - zeit, Ihr

müss - et ihm ent - ge - gen geh'n.

TEXT AND TRANSLATION

Wachet auf, ruft uns die Stimme,
Der Wächter sehr hoch auf der Zinne:
Wach auf, du Stadt Jerusalem!

Mitternacht heißt diese Stunde,
Sie rufen uns mit hellem Munde:
Wo seid ihr klugen Jungfrauen?

Wohl auf, der Bräut'gam kommt,
Steht auf, die Lampen nehmt!
Halleluia!

Macht euch bereit
Zu der Hochzeit,
Ihr müsset ihm entgegen geh'n.

Wake up! the voice calls to us,
The watchman very high on the walls calls,
Wake up, city of Jerusalem!

Midnight this hour is called,
They call us with bright voices,
Where are you, clever young women?

Wake up, the bridegroom comes,
Stand up, take up the lamps!
Halleluia!

Make yourselves ready
For the wedding.
You must go out to meet him.

Johann Sebastian Bach

Chorale Prelude on "Wachet auf" (Schübler chorale)

This prelude is part of a collection of six chorale preludes (contrapuntal embellishments of chorale tunes) by Bach that were engraved and published by Johann Georg Schübler and appeared in the late 1740s. Based on the chorale "Wachet auf" (p. 26), the piece is an organ transcription of a movement from the cantata of the same name. The chorale tune appears, in a relatively unadorned form, beginning in measure 13 in the organist's left hand.

Johann Sebastian Bach
Inventions

Around 1720, Bach composed a number of two-voice contrapuntal keyboard works, called inventions, for his ten-year-old son, Wilhelm Friedemann; these include the Inventions in D Minor and F Major. Bach's inventions were intended to teach students how to play two simultaneous lines on the harpsichord and how to develop a musical idea in the course of a piece.

Invention in D Minor

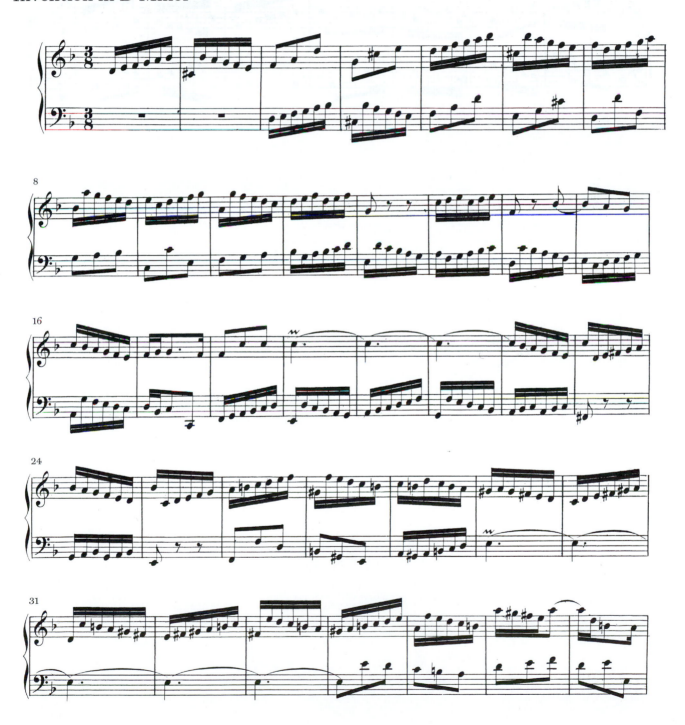

Invention in F Major

Johann Sebastian Bach
Fugue in E♭ Major for Organ (*St. Anne*), from *Clavierübung* III

The "St. Anne" Fugue, written in 1739, is one of Bach's most monumental and famous organ compositions. The name, which did not originate with Bach, refers to the initial melody's resemblance to the hymn tune "St. Anne" (p. 270). The Prelude and Fugue in E♭ Major are the opening and closing works to Bach's *Clavierübung*, Part III (the Prelude at the beginning and the Fugue at the end), which also includes twenty-one chorale preludes and four duets. The "St. Anne" Fugue has three distinct sections and three fugue subjects, two of which are combined at its climax.

Johann Sebastian Bach
Passacaglia in C Minor for Organ

Bach, who was better known during his lifetime as an organist than as a composer, wrote and performed the Passacaglia in C Minor between 1708 and 1712, when he was serving as organist at the St. Blasius Church in Mühlhausen. A passacaglia, a common genre of baroque keyboard music, consists of a series of variations over a repeated bass line. This famous passacaglia concludes with a double fugue (not given here) that is based on the same theme.

Johann Sebastian Bach

From Suites for Unaccompanied Cello

These movements are from two suites of dance pieces for solo cello, composed by J.S. Bach around 1720, when he was serving as the director of court music at Cöthen. During his years there, Bach focused his energy on secular instrumental music and wrote numerous suites, including six for solo cello. Suites represent one of the most important instrumental genres of the Baroque period and consist of a series of stylized dance movements—often in binary form—such as allemandes, courantes, sarabandes, minuets, and gigues.

Minuet, from Cello Suite No. 1 in G Major

Prelude, from Cello Suite No. 2 in D Minor

Johann Sebastian Bach Prelude, from Cello Suite No. 2 in D Minor

Johann Sebastian Bach
From *The Well-Tempered Clavier*, Book I

The Well-Tempered Clavier consists of two books, published by Bach in 1722 and 1742, each containing twenty-four paired preludes and fugues, one pair in each major and minor key. "Well-tempered" refers to tuning; a well-tempered keyboard instrument is tuned such that it can be played in any key. A number of earlier tuning systems, or "temperaments," based on the pure tuning of particular intervals, were in use during Bach's life; in these temperaments, keys close to C major sounded pleasing, but modulation to distant keys introduced out-of-tune intervals. Only later, with acceptance of equal temperament, could all twenty-four keys be used equally.

Prelude in C Major

Fugue in C Minor

Prelude in C♯ Minor

Fugue in D♯ Minor

Fugue in G Minor

Samuel Barber (1910–1981)

"Sea-Snatch," from *Hermit Songs*

Samuel Barber wrote the song cycle *Hermit Songs* in 1952–53. The cycle's texts come from anonymous (and somewhat scandalous) poetry written in the margins of medieval manuscripts by monks. The work was premiered in 1953 at the Library of Congress by soprano Leontyne Price, with the composer at the piano.

Béla Bartók (1881–1945)
Bagatelle, Op. 6, No. 2

The *Bagatelles* are short piano pieces that Bartók composed in 1908. In these early works, Bartók explores many techniques that will become important to his later compositions, including ostinatos and changing meters (both seen here), and borrowed folk melodies.

Béla Bartók

From *Mikrokosmos*

"Bulgarian Rhythm," "From the Island of Bali," and "Whole-Tone Scale" appear in *Mikrokosmos*, a six-volume series for beginning to advanced pianists. These books were begun for Bartók's son Péter's piano instruction; published in 1940, they reflect Bartók's life-long interest in musical pedagogy. The works also form a compendium of the composer's compositional techniques, including asymmetrical and changing meters, unconventional key signatures and modal materials, use of Bulgarian and other folk materials, symmetrical musical structures, and rhythmic ostinatos.

"Bulgarian Rhythm" (No. 115)

"From the Isle of Bali" (No. 109)

"Whole-Tone Scale" (No. 136)

Béla Bartók
"Song of the Harvest," for two violins

The "Song of the Harvest" appears in a set of forty-four violin duets that Bartók assembled for the German violin teacher Erich Dofein. Like the *Mikrokosmos,* these duets are arranged in a pedagogical sequence from simplest to most difficult. They borrow from and imitate features of a number of Eastern European folk repertoires.

Ludwig van Beethoven (1770–1827)

Für Elise

This short work, one of Beethoven's most popular keyboard pieces, was not published until after his death. It is also known as the *Bagatelle* No. 25 in A Minor (cataloged as a work without opus number, WoO 59). Although there is much speculation, no one knows exactly who Elise was.

Ludwig van Beethoven
Piano Sonata in F Minor, Op. 2, No. 1, first movement

In 1792, Beethoven left his hometown of Bonn for Vienna, where, according to an early patron, he was to "receive Mozart's spirit through Haydn's hands." Once there, Beethoven studied counterpoint and composition with Haydn. Beethoven wrote this sonata in 1795 and dedicated it to his mentor.

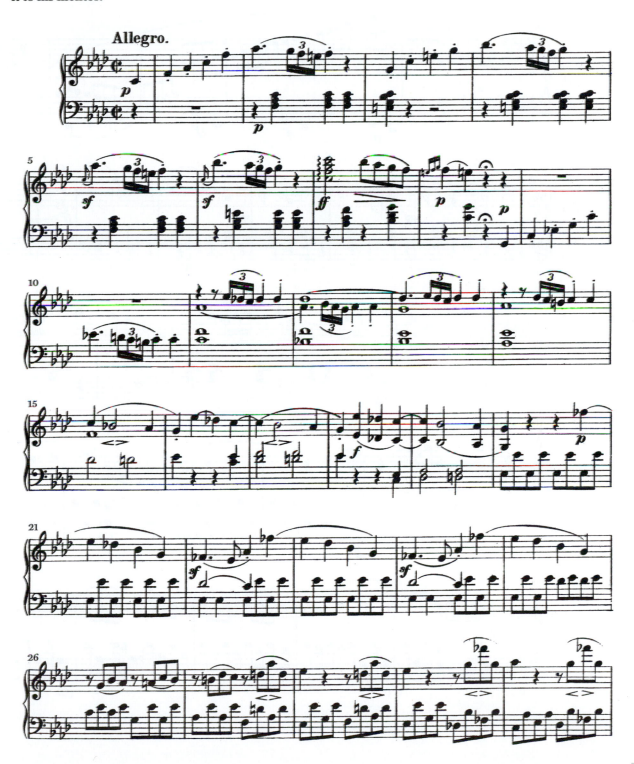

Ludwig van Beethoven
Piano Sonata in E♭ Major, Op. 7, second movement

During his lifetime, Beethoven supported himself by presenting public concerts and teaching. This sonata, written in 1796, was composed for Beethoven's student Anna Louise Barbara Keglevich, a countess in a Croatian noble family.

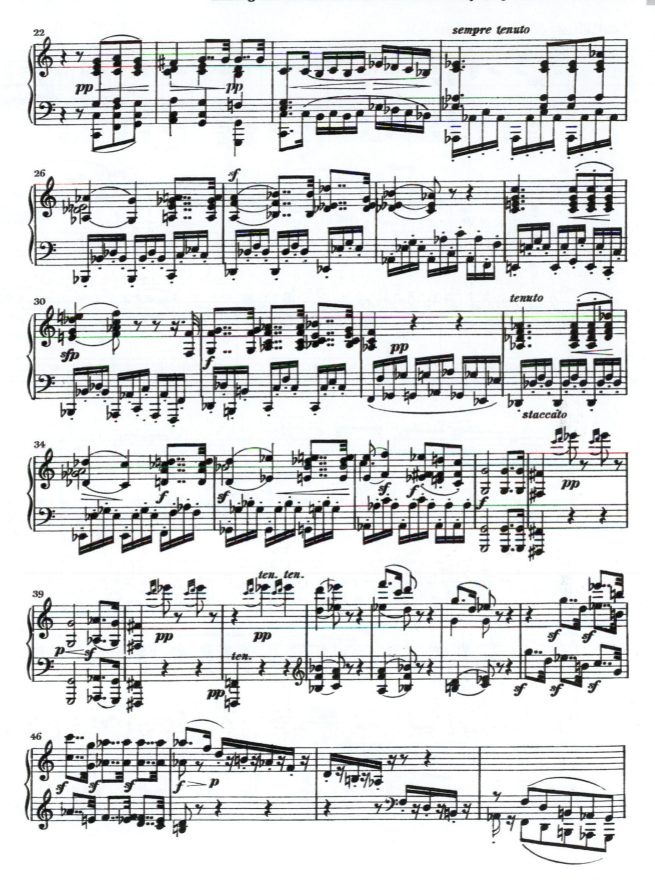

Ludwig van Beethoven
Piano Sonata in C Minor, Op. 13 (*Pathétique*)

Beethoven composed the *Pathétique* Sonata in 1799, at age twenty-seven, during his first decade composing and performing in Vienna. The subtitle, *Pathétique*, which would have appealed to nineteenth-century audiences, means "with pathos." The work was dedicated to Prince Karl von Lichnowsky, who was a supporter and patron to both Mozart and Beethoven. In the recordings that accompany this anthology, the second movement is performed on fortepiano, an early keyboard from Beethoven's era. The first and third movements, for comparison, are played on a modern piano.

Attacca subito l' Allegro:

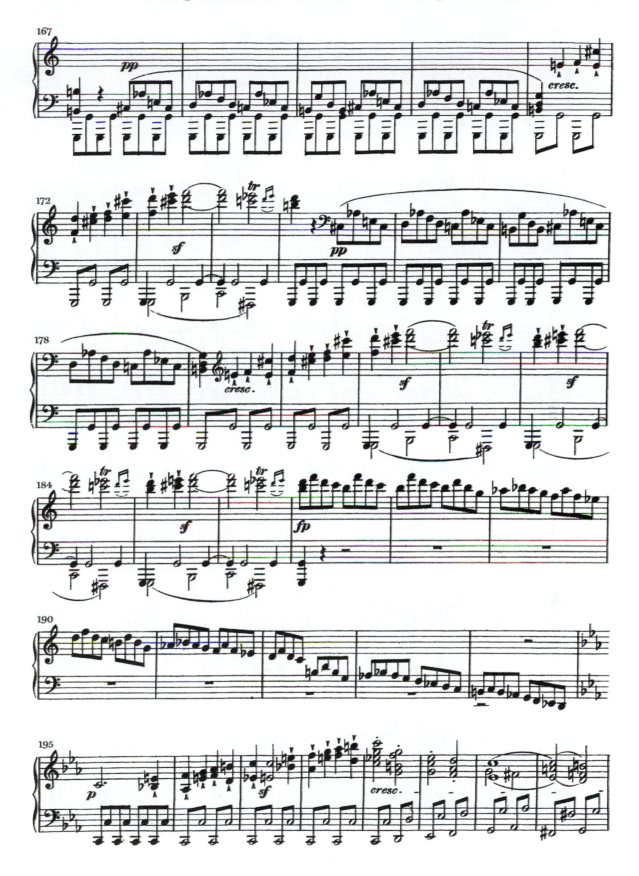

Adagio cantabile.

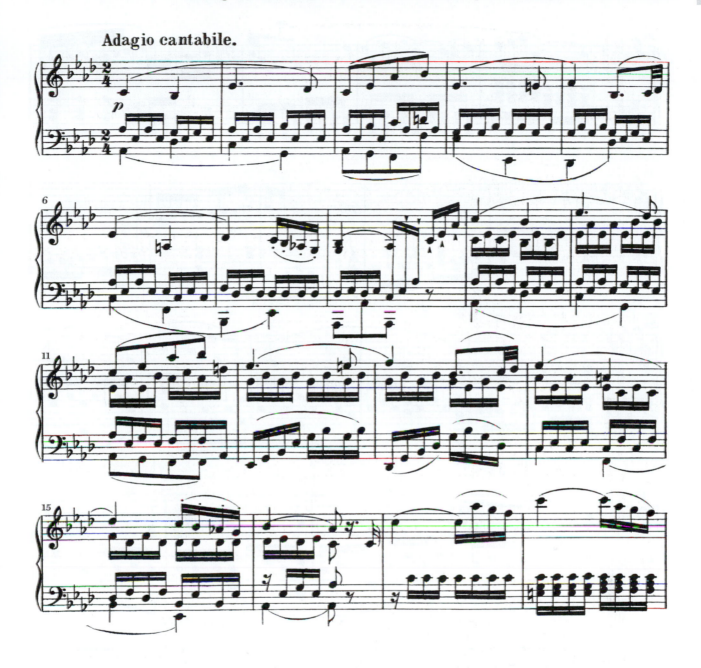

Ludwig van Beethoven
Piano Sonata in C Major, Op. 53 (*Waldstein*),
first movement

The *Waldstein* Sonata exemplifies the second of the three periods into which historians frequently divide Beethoven's work. The middle period is sometimes known as the "heroic" period, during which Beethoven composed Symphonies 3 through 8 and some of his most famous piano sonatas (including also the *Moonlight* and *Appassionata*). Composed in 1805, this sonata takes its name from Beethoven's friend and supporter Count Ferdinand von Waldstein, to whom it is dedicated.

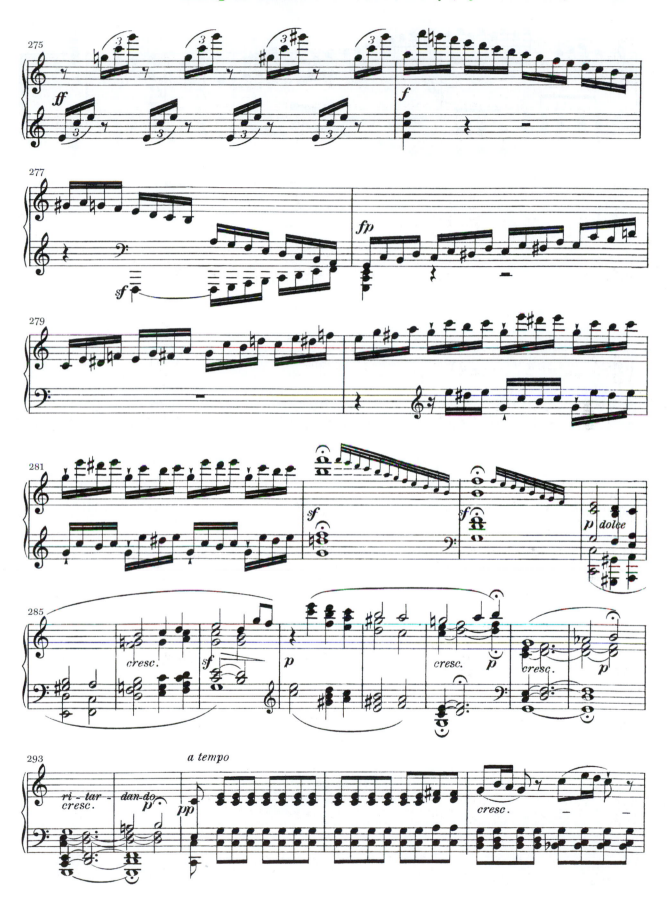

Ludwig van Beethoven
Sonatina in F Major, Op. Posth., second movement

Beethoven composed several sonatinas, or brief sonatas, before making the substantial journey from his birthplace, Bonn, to the cultural capital of the German-speaking world, Vienna. The Sonatina in F, composed between 1790 and 1792, was not published during his lifetime.

Ludwig van Beethoven

Seven Variations on "God Save the King"

This work, as well as a set of variations on the tune "Rule Britannia," both came out of Beethoven's correspondence with Scottish folklorist George Thomson in 1802. Thomson later persuaded Beethoven to harmonize a number of British folk songs.

Alban Berg (1885–1935)
"Sahst du nach dem Gewitterregen," from
Fünf Orchester-Lieder (reduction)

"Sahst du nach dem Gewitterregen" ("Did You See, After the Summer Rain") comes from a collection of songs for voice and orchestra first performed in 1913 at a concert conducted by Arnold Schoenberg. The fragmentary texts used in the songs were written by poet Peter Altenberg on the backs of postcards, and evoke conditions of the soul.

Text by Peter Altenberg

TEXT AND TRANSLATION

Sahst du nach dem Gewitterregen den Wald?
Alles rastet, blinkt und ist schöner als zuvor.
Siehe, Fraue, auch du brauchst Gewitterregen!

Did you see, after the summer rain, the forest?
All is quiet, sparkling, and more beautiful than before.
See, woman, you too need summer rainstorms!

Johannes Brahms (1833–1897)
"Die Mainacht"

Brahms set "Die Mainacht" ("The May Night"), by the eighteenth-century German poet Ludwig Hölty, in 1866. The text, filled with images of nature, was also set by Franz Schubert and Fanny Hensel.

Text by Ludwig Christoph Heinrich Hölty

TEXT AND TRANSLATION

"Die Mainacht"

Wann der silberne Mond durch die Gesträuche blinkt,
Und sein schlummerndes Licht über den Rasen streut,
Und die Nachtigall flötet,
Wandl' ich traurig von Busch zu Busch.

Überhüllet vom Laub girret ein Taubenpaar
Sein Entzücken mir vor; aber ich wende mich,
Suche dunklere Schatten,
Und die einsame Träne rinnt.

Wann, o lächelndes Bild, welches wie Morgenrot
Durch sie Seele mir strahlt, find ich auf Erden dich?
Und die einsame Träne
Bebt mir heisser die Wang herab!

"The May Night"

When the silvery moon beams through the shrubbery,
And its slumbering light scatters over the lawn,
And the nightingale flutes,
I wander sadly from bush to bush.

Veiled by leaves, a pair of doves coo
Their delight in front of me, but I turn,
Seeking darker shadows,
And the lonely tear runs down.

When, O smiling image, who shines like rosy dawn
Through my soul, shall I find you on earth?
And the lonely tear
Trembles, burning, down my cheek.

Johannes Brahms
Intermezzo in A Major, Op. 118, No. 2

The Intermezzo in A Major, published in 1893, comes from one of four collections of short piano pieces that Brahms compiled during the last decade of his life. The title "Intermezzo" was first used in the Renaissance to describe short musical interludes that separated acts of a play. By the nineteenth century, the term had come to mean a short, lyrical instrumental composition, most often for piano.

Johannes Brahms
Variations on a Theme by Haydn, theme (two pianos)

Over the course of his life, Brahms wrote numerous sets of variations on themes by other composers, including Schumann, Handel, and Paganini. The *Variations on a Theme by Haydn*, written in 1873, takes the "St. Anthony" Chorale, once believed to be by Haydn, as its theme. Brahms prepared two versions of the piece: the one for two pianos that appears here and another for orchestra.

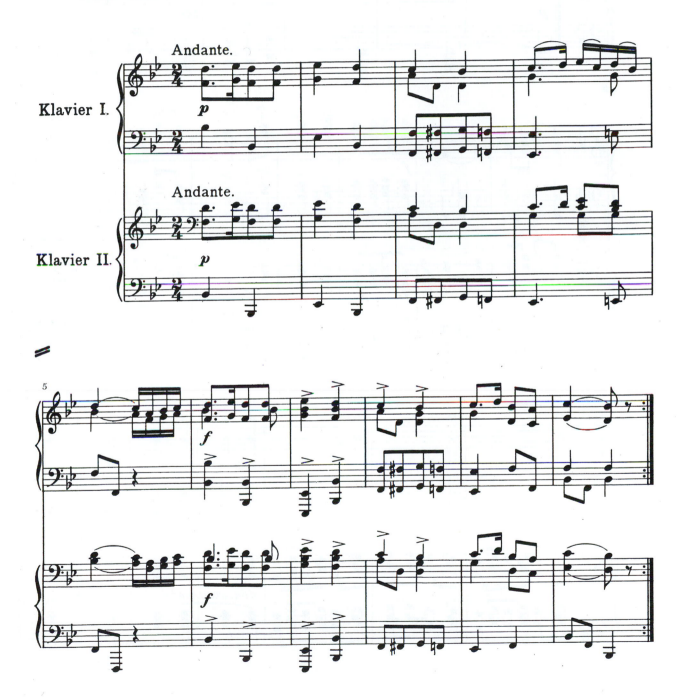

Frédéric Chopin (1810–1849)
Mazurka in F Minor, Op. 68, No. 4

A mazurka is a dance in triple meter that originated in the Mazovia region of Poland and by the nineteenth century had become popular all over Europe. Chopin, who grew up in the Mazovia region, composed numerous mazurkas. This one, sketched in 1846 and published after his death, was one of his last contributions to the genre.

Frédéric Chopin
Nocturne in E♭ Major, Op. 9, No. 2

Chopin included the Nocturne in E♭ Major in a set of nocturnes published in 1832, shortly after he had left his native Poland. A nocturne is a composition intended to invoke the sounds or feeling of the night. Chopin composed numerous nocturnes, consisting of slow, songlike melodies that are accompanied by arpeggiated chords, often simulating a guitar.

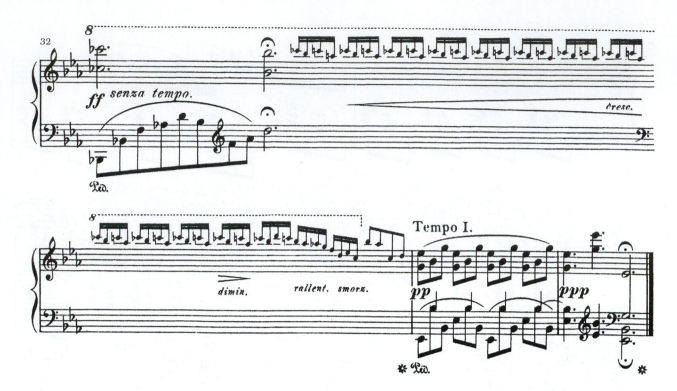

Frédéric Chopin
Prelude in C Minor, Op. 28, No. 20

This piece is included in a collection of short preludes that Chopin composed in 1839. Like each volume of Bach's *Well-Tempered Clavier* (p. 55), which Chopin was studying when he wrote his own preludes, Op. 28 consists of one prelude in each of the twenty-four major and minor keys. Unlike Bach's, however, Chopin's preludes are not paired with fugues.

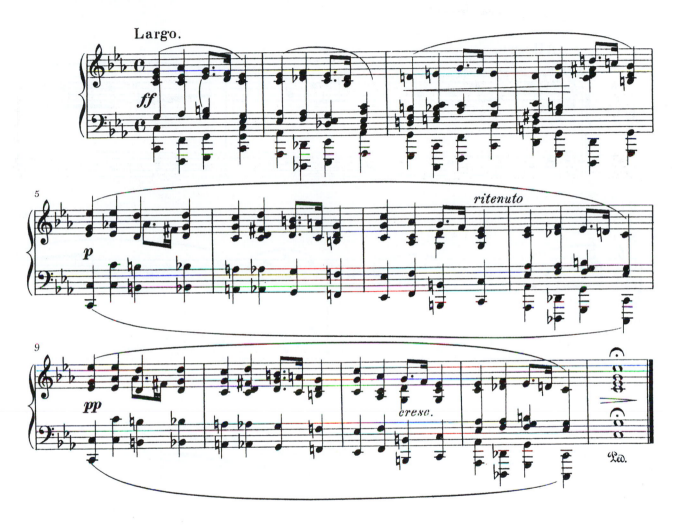

Muzio Clementi (1752–1832)

Sonatina in C Major, Op. 36, No. 1, first movement

Clementi, a renowned piano virtuoso and teacher, published these sonatinas in 1797. Both were part of a supplement to *Introduction to the Art of Playing on the Piano Forte*, an instructional handbook for pianists. Even today, Clementi's sonatinas are important to piano instruction and are reprinted in a number of collections of short works for intermediate-level students.

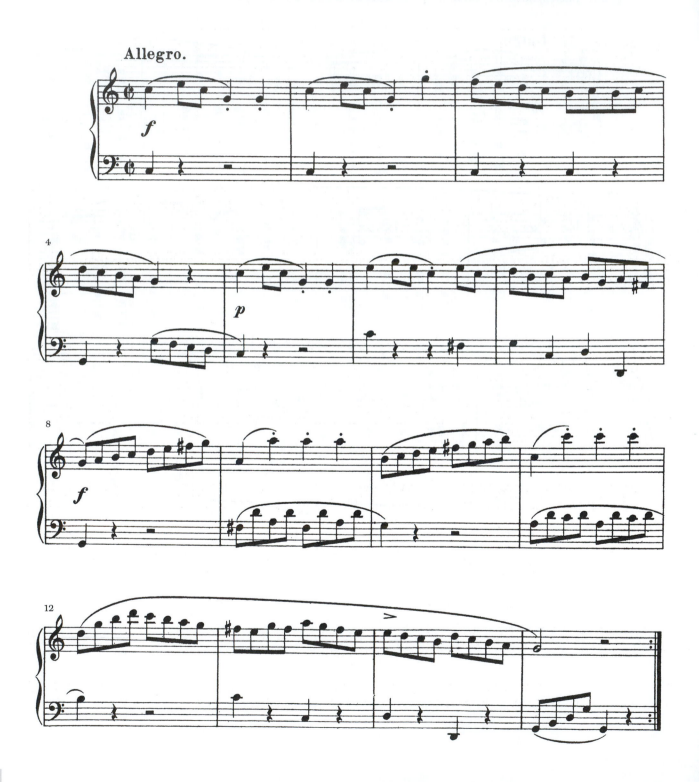

Muzio Clementi
Sonatina in F Major, Op. 36, No. 4, first movement

Arcangelo Corelli (1653–1713)
Allemanda, from Trio Sonata in A Minor, Op. 4, No. 5

This Allemanda comes from a trio sonata for two violins and continuo instruments, written in 1694 by the Italian composer Arcangelo Corelli. *Sonate da camera* (secular chamber sonatas, as opposed to church sonatas), like Corelli's Op. 4, No. 5, consisted of a series of dance movements. A blank staff is added to the score here for practice writing a continuo realization.

Arcangelo Corelli
Preludio, from Sonata in D Minor, Op. 4, No. 8

This Preludio is the first movement of a trio sonata composed in 1694. Despite its name, a trio sonata requires four players for a performance: two soloists (in this case, violinists), a third performer to play the bass line, and a fourth to fill out the harmonies by realizing the figured bass (on an instrument such as the harpsichord). A blank staff is added to the score here for practice writing a continuo realization.

John Corigliano (b. 1938)

"Come now, my darling," from *The Ghosts of Versailles*

The Ghosts of Versailles received its premiere in 1991 at the Metropolitan Opera in New York. Its plot revolves around an opera-within-an-opera, staged by the French playwright Pierre Beaumarchais for the ghosts of the French court of Louis XVI and Marie Antoinette. The characters who sing this duet, the Countess Rosina and Cherubino, also figure prominently in Mozart's opera *The Marriage of Figaro* (p. 288).

Libretto by William M. Hoffman

Soprano (Rosina): Where are you tak-ing me, young shep-herd?

Mezzo-soprano (Cherubino): Look at the green here in the glade.

M-s Feel the mild breeze and the scent_ of wild thyme. Hear the vix-en's shrill cry and the lamb's com-plaint.

Let us strew the bed ___ with flow - ers, There ___ we will spend the hours. ___

poco rall.

There we will spend the hours. _____ There we will spend the hours.

A tempo

Yes, yes, my dar - ling, I'll come with thee, Come to the room that is made for me.

Come now, my dar - ling, come with me, Come to the room I have

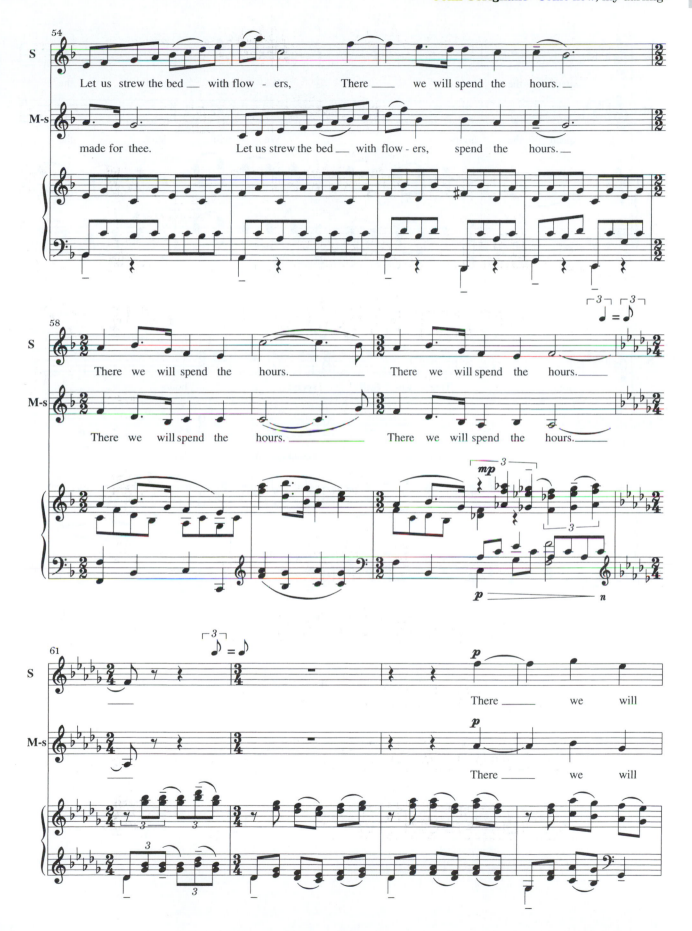

Luigi Dallapiccola (1904–1975)

"Die Sonne kommt!," from *Goethe-lieder*, for voice and clarinets

Dallapiccola's *Goethe-lieder*, a work influenced by the twelve-tone music of Anton Webern, was composed in 1953 to texts by Johann Wolfgang von Goethe, whom many consider to be Germany's greatest poet. For an example of another Goethe setting, see Schubert's "Erlkönig" (p. 410).

Text by Johann Wolfgang von Goethe

*The part for piccolo clarinet is written at sounding pitch.

TEXT AND TRANSLATION

Die Sonne kommt! Ein Prachterscheinen!	The sun comes up! A glorious sight!
Der Sichelmond umklammert sie.	The crescent moon embraces her.
Wer konnte solch ein Paar vereinen?	Who could unite such a pair?
Dies Rätsel, wie erklärt sich's? wie?	This riddle, how to solve it? How?

Claude Debussy (1862–1918)

"La cathédrale engloutie," from *Préludes*, Book I

"La cathédrale engloutie" ("The Engulfed Cathedral") is included in Debussy's first book of preludes, published in 1910, a collection of short programmatic piano pieces. Debussy's preludes, unlike earlier keyboard collections like Bach's *Well-Tempered Clavier* (p. 55) and Chopin's Preludes (p. 159), do not cycle through all the keys, but instead focus on poetic titles and musical imagery. The title of this prelude refers to a Breton legend of an underwater cathedral that sometimes rises to the ocean's surface.

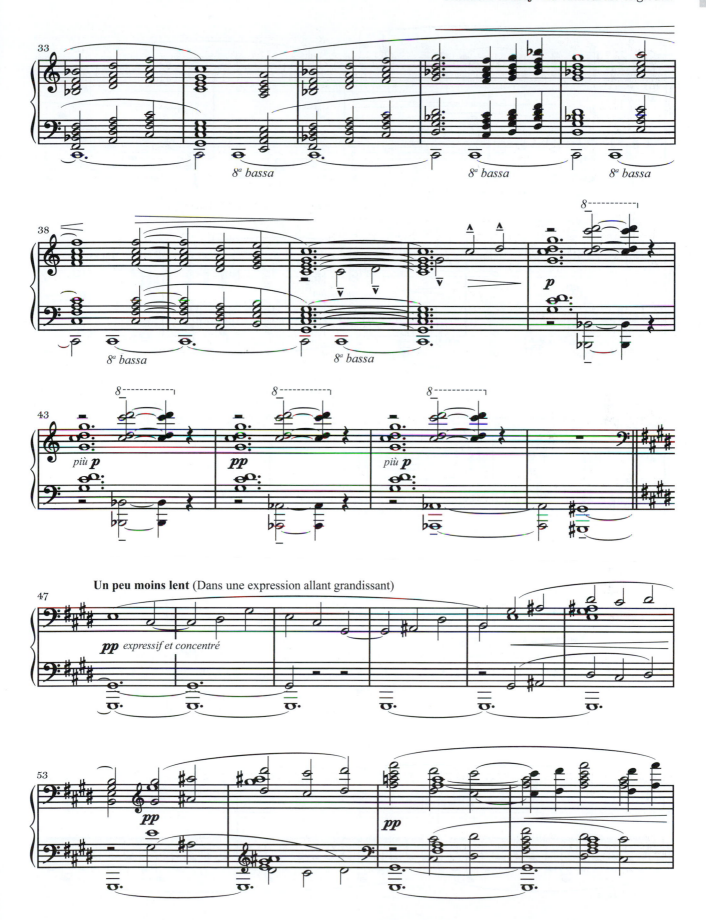

Claude Debussy
"Fantoches," from *Fêtes galantes*

Debussy's *Fêtes galantes* is a song cycle, written in 1869, setting texts by the poet Paul Verlaine. Verlaine's poetry is based on the *commedia dell'arte*, a tradition of improvising drama with stock characters. "Fantoches" ("Puppets") features several characters, including Scaramouche, Pulcinella, Il Dottore (the doctor)—a pompous, self-proclaimed learned character who wears a black mask—and his scandalous daughter, who sneaks out for an amorous encounter with a Spanish pirate.

Text by Paul Verlaine

un a _ mou _ reux ros _ si _ gnol _____ Cla _ me la dé _ tresse à tuc _

tê _____ te.

la la _____

la. _____

TEXT AND TRANSLATION

"Fantoches"

Scaramouche et Pulcinella
Qu'un mauvais dessein rassembla
Gesticulent noirs sous la lune.

Cependant l'excellent docteur
Bolonais cueille avec lenteur
Des simples parmi l'herbe brune.

Lors sa fille, piquant minois,
Sous la charmille, en tapinois,
Se glisse demi nue, en quête

De son beau pirate espagnol
Dont un amoureux rossignol
Clame la détresse à tue-tête.

"Puppets"

Scaramouche and Pulcinella
For an evil plan assembled
Gesticulate, black, under the moon.

Meanwhile, the excellent doctor
From Bologna picks slowly
By himself through the brown grass.

Then his daughter, with a spicy little face,
Under the hedgerow, stealthily
Slips, semi-nude, in search

Of her handsome Spanish pirate
For whom an amorous nightingale
Proclaims his distress loudly.

Gabriel Fauré (1845–1924)

"Après un rêve"

"Après un rêve" ("After a Dream"), composed in 1877, is one of many art songs by Fauré, who is regarded as one of the most significant composers of French art song, or mélodie. The text, by an anonymous Tuscan poet and translated into French by Romain Bussine, recalls a dreamed encounter with a lover.

TEXT AND TRANSLATION

"Après un rêve"

"After a Dream"

Dans un sommeil que charmait ton image
Je rêvais le bonheur, ardent mirage,
Tes yeux étaient plus doux, ta voix pure et sonore,
Tu rayonnais comme un ciel éclairé par l'aurore;

In a sleep that your image charmed,
I dreamed of happiness, ardent mirage,
Your eyes were softer, your voice pure and sonorous,
You shone like a sky lit by the dawn;

Tu m'appelais et je quittais la terre
Pour m'enfuir avec toi vers la lumière,
Les cieux pour nous entr'ouvraient leurs nues,
Splendeurs inconnues, lueurs divines entrevues,

You called me and I left the earth
To run away with you toward the light,
The skies parted their clouds for us,
Splendors unknown, divine light glimpsed,

Hélas! Hélas! triste réveil des songes
Je t'appelle, ô nuit, rends moi tes mensonges,
Reviens, reviens radieuse,
Reviens ô nuit mystérieuse!

Alas, alas, sad awakening from the dreams,
I call you, O night, give me back your lies,
Return, return radiant,
Return, O mysterious night!

Stephen Foster (1826–1864)
"Jeanie with the Light Brown Hair"

Stephen Foster was a prolific songwriter of the mid-nineteenth century, whose songs, in addition to "Jeanie with the Light Brown Hair," include "Old Folks at Home," "Beautiful Dreamer," "Oh! Susanna," and "Camptown Races." In this song, "Jeanie" is Jane McDowell, Foster's wife.

Stephen Foster

"Oh! Susanna"

This song, published in 1848, exemplifies the style of Stephen Foster, whose parlor and minstrel songs achieved enormous popularity in his day. In fact, many of his songs continue to be so well known that they are assumed to be folk songs rather than nineteenth-century compositions. Although some of Foster's songs seem to glorify the slavery and plantations of the Old South, he was born in Pittsburgh and only visited the South once.

2. It rained all day the night I left
   The weather was so dry;
   The sun so hot I froze myself,
   Susanna, don't you cry.
   Chorus

3. I had a dream the other night,
   When everything was still.
   I thought I saw Susanna
   A-coming down the hill.
   Chorus

4. The buckwheat cake was in her mouth,
   The tear was in her eye,
   Says I, "I'm coming from the South."
   Susanna, don't you cry.
   Chorus

George Gershwin (1898–1937)
"I Got Rhythm," from *Girl Crazy*

George and Ira Gershwin were composer-lyricist brothers, who wrote "I Got Rhythm" for a Broadway musical, *Girl Crazy,* in 1930. The song's chord progression, known as its "changes," has served as the basis for numerous jazz compositions, including works by Duke Ellington, Dizzy Gillespie, and Thelonious Monk.

Lyrics by Ira Gershwin

George Frideric Handel (1685–1759)

Chaconne in G Major

This Chaconne, a revised version of a composition Handel wrote in 1705, appeared in a collection of his harpsichord music published in 1733. Handel lived in an era without copyright laws, and he produced the 1733 collection to compete with pirated editions of his works (including the Chaconne) that were already in circulation. Like all chaconnes, Handel's consists of variations on a repeated harmonic pattern.

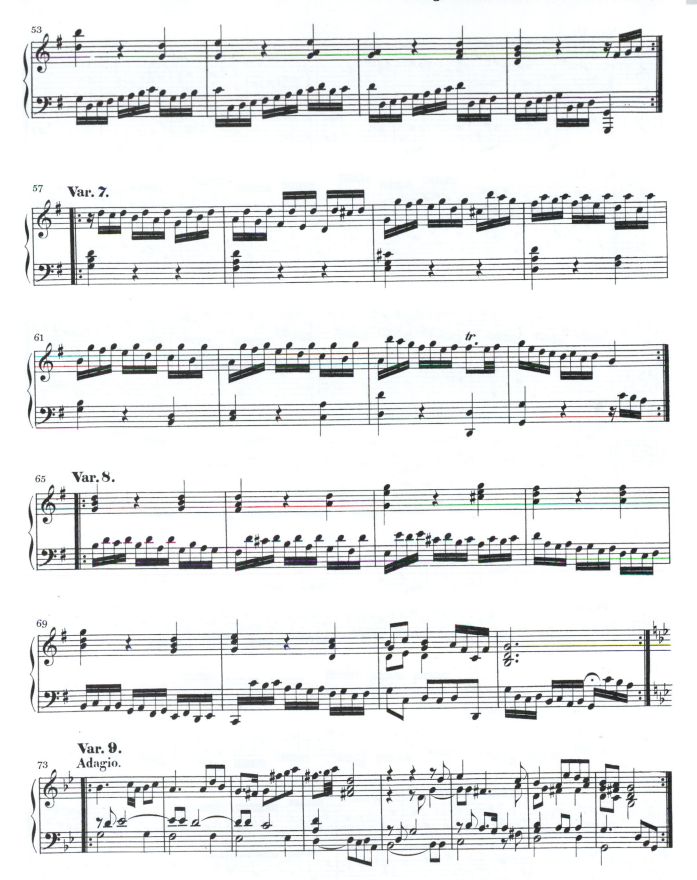

George Frideric Handel

From *Messiah*

Handel's *Messiah,* composed in 1741, is an example of an oratorio—an unstaged, usually sacred vocal work that tells a story. After studying in Italy, the German-born Handel began his career in London as an opera composer, writing popular Italian operas; by the 1740s, tastes had shifted and he turned his attention to oratorios. *Messiah* tells the story of the life of Jesus, using texts from the Christian Bible. It is one of the most widely performed oratorios today, with numerous choral organizations presenting annual performances (often in abridged versions). Two solo movements are shown next: an aria for soprano and a recitative for tenor.

"Rejoice greatly"

be - hold,__ thy__ king__ com-eth un - to__ thee,__ com-eth

un - to thee.

he is_____ the right - eous Sav - ior,   and he shall

speak,   he shall speak peace,   peace,_____

____ he shall speak   peace_____ un - to   the   hea -

then.   Re - joice,   re -

a tempo

f   *p*

"Thy rebuke hath broken His heart"

Joseph Haydn (1732–1809)
Concerto in D Major for Corno di caccia and Orchestra, first movement

Haydn wrote this concerto for corno di caccia—or hunting horn—and orchestra in 1762. Since valves had not yet been invented, this work was written for a natural horn—an instrument without valves. By changing the speed of the column of air moving through the instrument, performers can change pitches within the harmonic series. Changing the position of the right hand within the bell allows the performer to play other pitches.

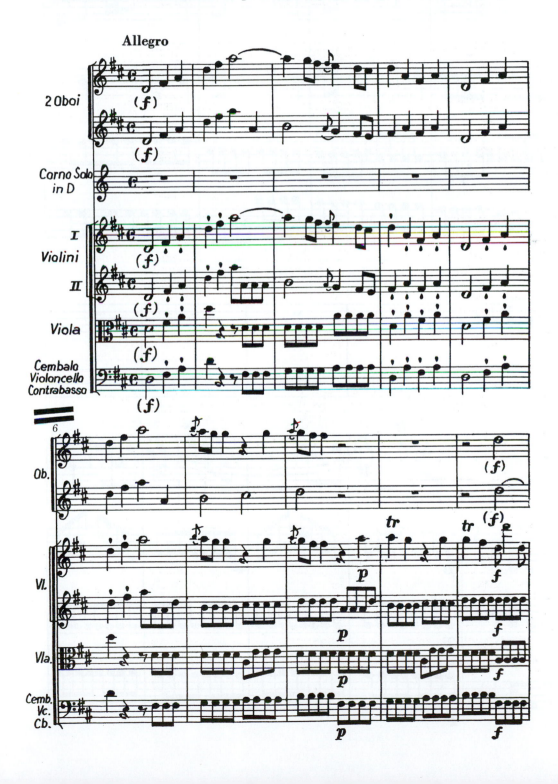

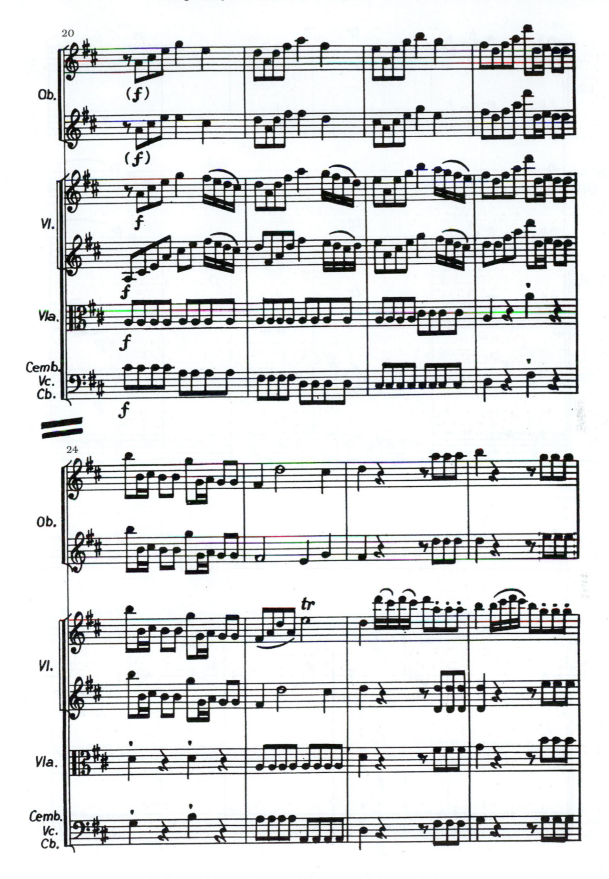

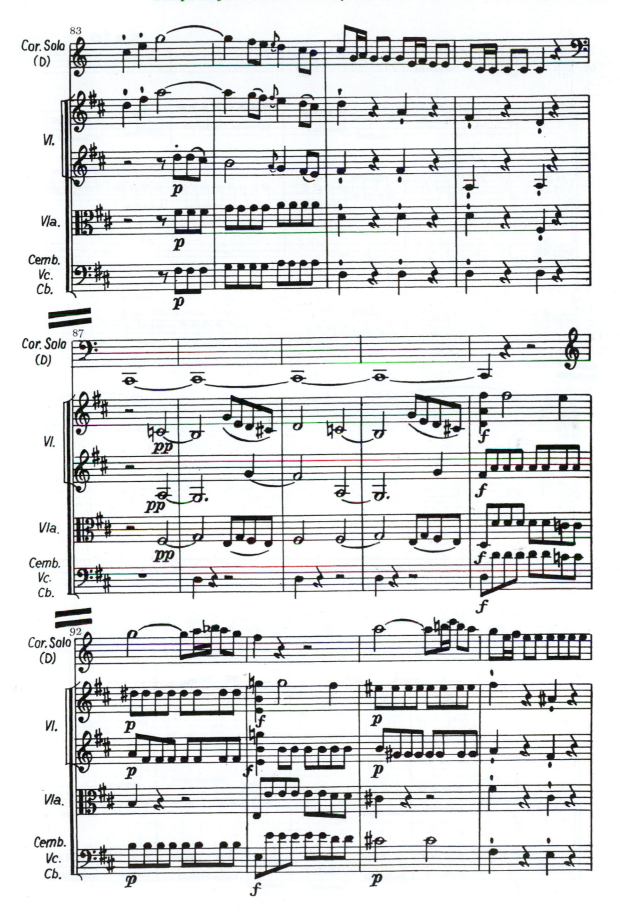

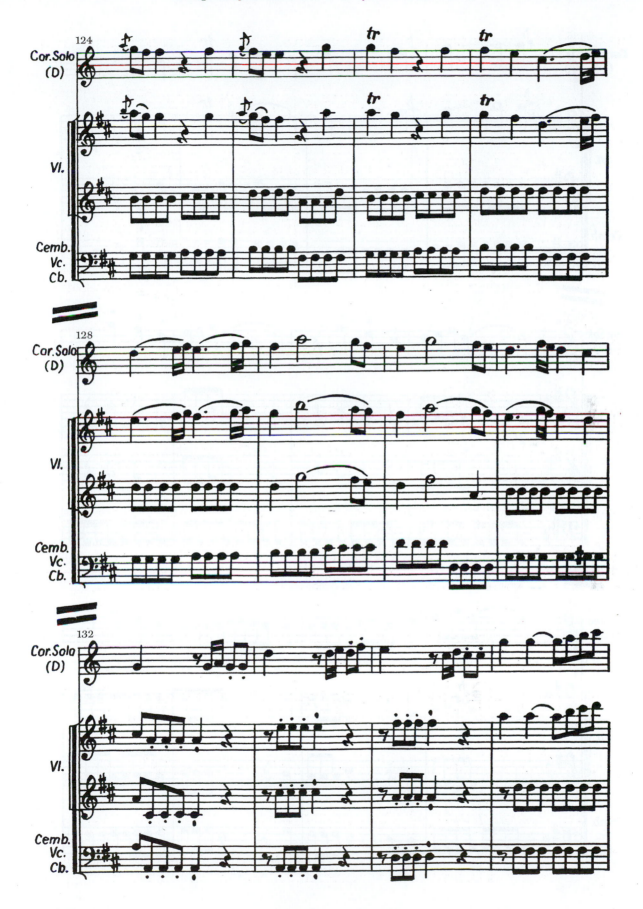

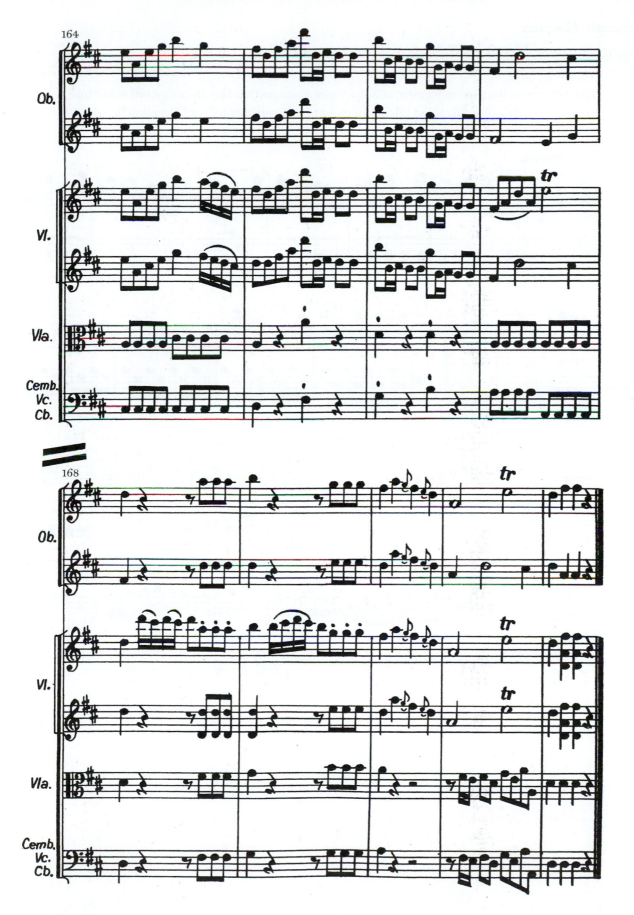

Joseph Haydn
Piano Sonata No. 9 in F Major, third movement

This Scherzo is the final movement of a short piano sonata that Haydn composed sometime before 1766. He originally titled this simple sonata a "divertimento" (or "diversion").

Joseph Haydn
Menuetto and Trio, from String Quartet in D Minor, Op. 76, No. 2 (*Quinten*)

Haydn was one of the first composers to write for string quartet, a genre to which he frequently returned, publishing numerous collections of quartets. The *Quinten* ("Fifths") Quartet is part of a collection published in 1797. Its name comes from the quartet's first movement, which makes prominent use of perfect fifths. The menuetto is unusual in that it combines a contrapuntal technique, a strict canon, with a Classical binary form.

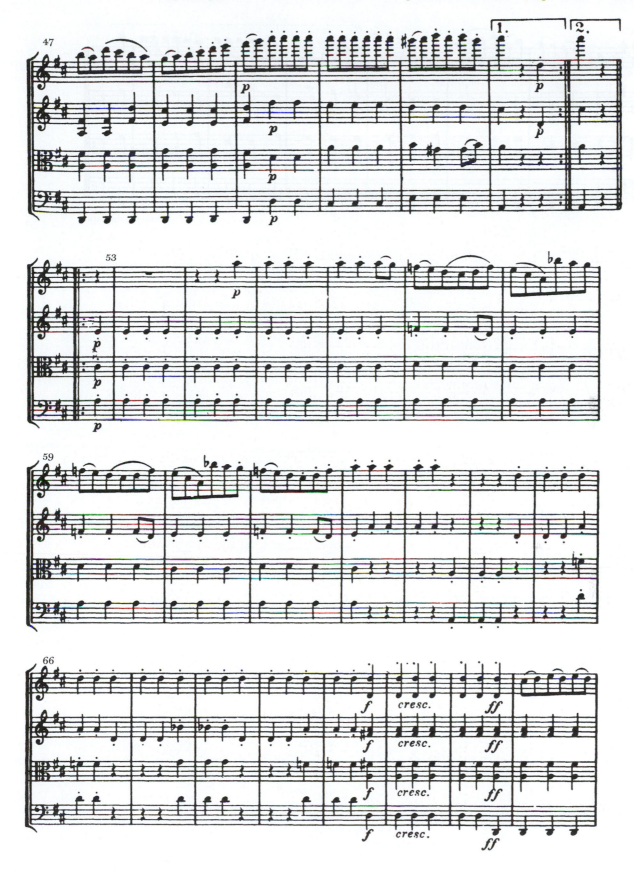

Menuetto da Capo

Fanny Mendelssohn Hensel (1805–1847)

"Nachtwanderer"

Fanny Mendelssohn Hensel and her brother, Felix Mendelssohn, were raised in a musical household. Fanny was encouraged to compose by her brother, whose works she influenced. Because there were few publication opportunities for women composers, Hensel published some of her songs under her brother's name, but in 1846, near the end of her life, she published one volume of Lieder in her own name. "Nachtwanderer" appears in a collection of songs by Hensel published in 1848, a year after her death. It is a setting of a poem by Joseph Karl Benedikt von Eichendorff, a German lyric poet whose writings were often set by composers.

Text by Joseph Karl Benedikt von Eichendorff

Andante con moto

Ich wand - re durch die stil - le Nacht, da schleicht der Mond so heim - lich sacht oft aus der dun - keln Wol - - - - ken - hül - - le.

Und hin und her im Tal er - wacht die Nach - ti -

gall, dann wie - der al - les grau, al - les

grau_____ und stil - - le. O

wun - der - ba - rer Nacht - ge - sang,_____ von fern im Land der Strö - me Gang,

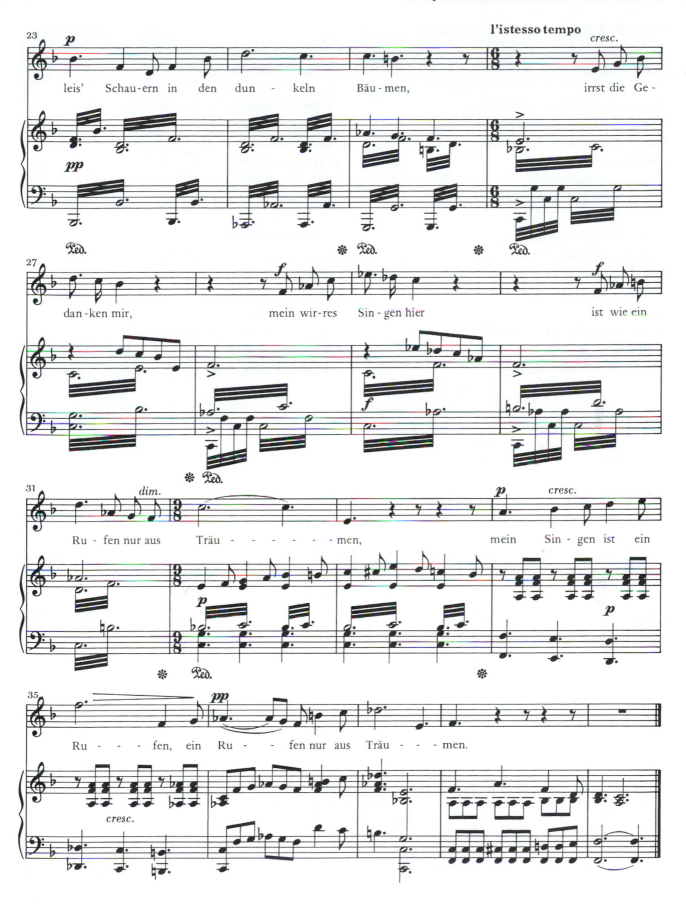

TEXT AND TRANSLATION

"Nachtwanderer"

Ich wandre durch die stille Nacht,
Da schleicht der Mond so heimlich sacht
Oft aus der dunkeln Wolkenhülle.
Und hin und her im Tal
Erwacht die Nachtigall,
Dann wieder alles grau und stille.

O wunderbarer Nachtgesang,
Von fern im Land der Ströme Gang,
Leis' Schauern in den dunkeln Bäumen,
Irrst die Gedanken mir,
Mein wirres Singen hier
Ist wie ein Rufen nur aus Träumen,
Mein Singen is ein Rufen,
Ein Rufen nur aus Träumen.

"Night Wanderer"

I wander through the still night;
There creeps the moon so secretly, gently,
Often out from the dark cloud cover.
And here and there in the valley
Wakes the nightingale,
Then again all is gray and still.

O wonderful night song,
From afar in the land where the currents flow,
Soft shuddering in the dark trees
Confuses my thoughts.
My wild singing here
Is like a cry only from dreams;
My singing is a cry,
A cry only from dreams.

Fanny Mendelssohn Hensel

"Neue Liebe, neues Leben"

"Neue Liebe, neues Leben" ("New Love, New Life"), a setting of a poem by Johann Wolfgang
von Goethe, is one of many songs by Hensel that were unpublished during her lifetime.
Compare this lush Romantic setting with a Classical-style setting by Beethoven (his Op. 75,
No. 2), which presents a strikingly different interpretation of this text.

Text by Johann Wolfgang von Goethe

laß, oh _ laß _ mich los!

TEXT AND TRANSLATION

"Neue Liebe, neues Leben"

"New Love, New Life"

Herz, mein Herz, was soll das geben?
Was bedränget dich so sehr?
Welch' ein fremdes neues Leben,
Ich erkenne dich nicht mehr.

Heart, my heart, what does this mean?
What troubles you so much?
What a strange new life!
I don't recognize you anymore.

Weg ist alles, was du liebtest,
Weg, worum du dich betrübtest,
Weg dein Fleiß und deine Ruh',
Ach, wie kamst du nur dazu?

Gone is all that you loved,
Gone is what troubled you,
Gone your hard work and your peace,
Ah, how did you come to this?

Fesselt dich die Jugendblüte,
Diese liebliche Gestalt,
Dieser Blick voll Treu' und Güte,
Mit unendlicher Gewalt?

Are you captivated by youth's bloom,
This lovely form,
This gaze full of faithfulness and goodness,
With infinite power?

Will ich rasch mich ihr entziehen,
Mich ermannen, ihr entfliehen,
Führet mich im Augenblick
Ach, mein Weg zu ihr zurück.

If I swiftly run away from her
To take courage, to flee from her,
At that moment,
Ah, my way leads me back to her.

Und an diesem Zauberfädchen,
Das sich nicht zerreißen läßt,
Hält das liebe, lose Mädchen
Mich so wider Willen fest;

And with this magic thread,
Which cannot be cut,
The sweet, mischievous maiden
Holds me so tightly against my will;

Muß in ihrem Zauberkreise
Leben nun auf ihre Weise.
[Die Verändrung], ach wie groß,
Liebe, Liebe, laß mich los!

I must in her magic circle
Live now in her manner.
[The transformation], oh how great,
Love, love, let me go!

Gustav Holst (1874–1934)
Second Suite for Military Band in F Major, fourth movement ("Fantasia on the 'Dargason'")

In his Second Suite for Military Band, written in 1911, Holst borrowed a number of old tunes, mostly from folk and dance music. This last movement of the suite makes use of a sixteenth-century English dance song called "Dargason" and the folk tune "Greensleeves." Sources differ on the origin of the name "Dargason," variously associating it with a legendary Irish monster that resembled a large bear, or the Anglo-Saxon word for a fairy. At the climax of the movement, the two tunes are combined.

Condensed/conductor score

Full band score, mm. 1–56

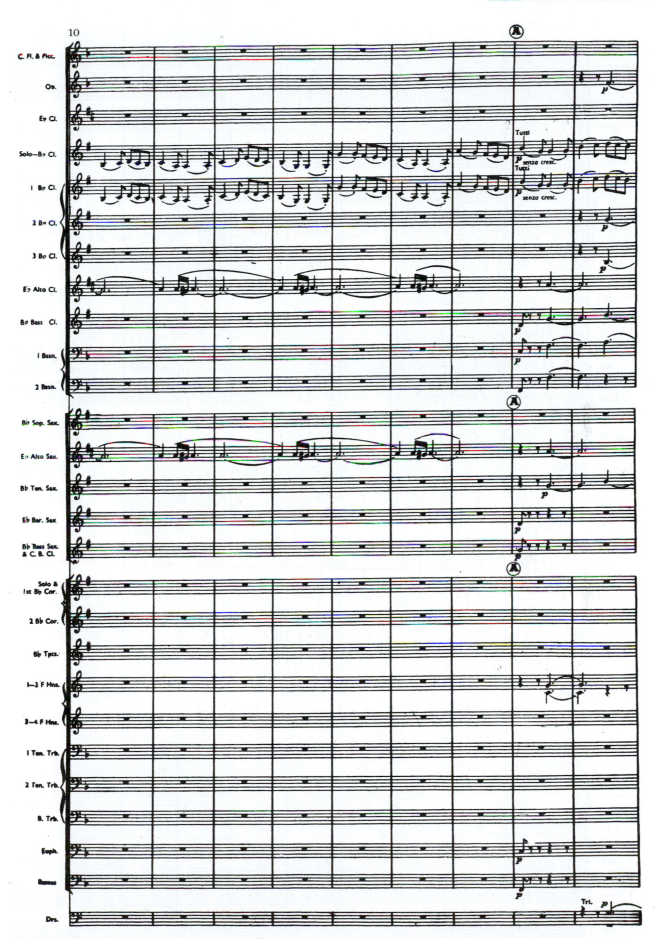

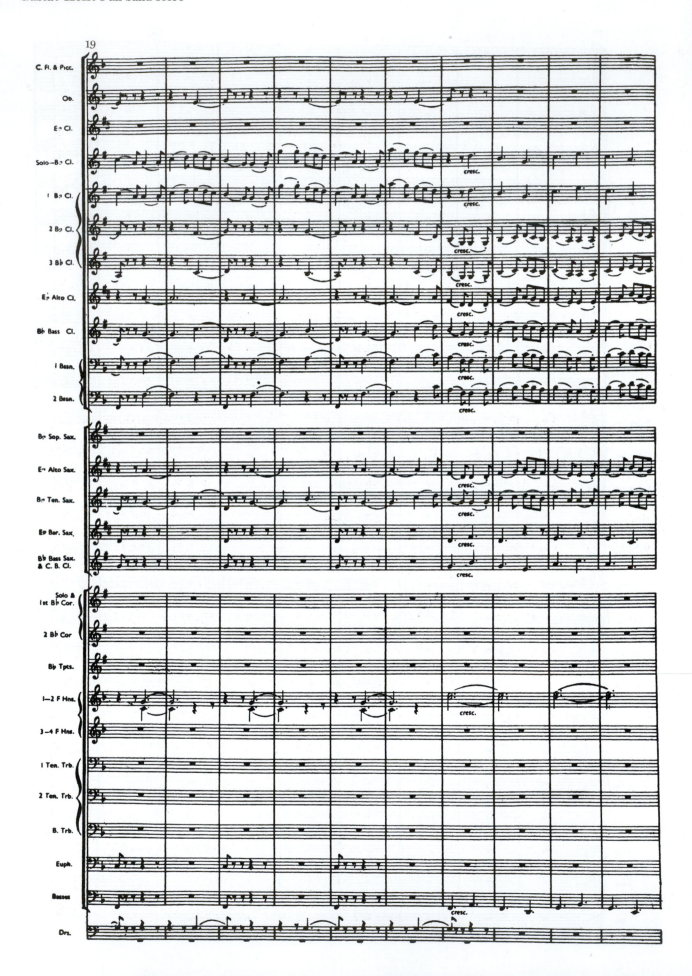

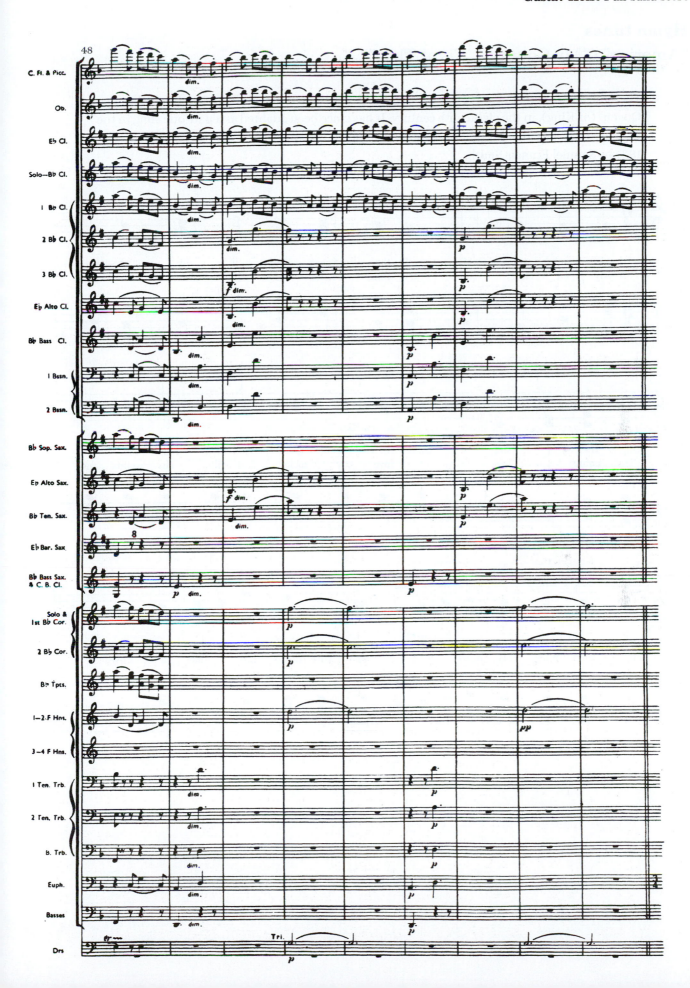

Hymn tunes
"America" ("My Country, 'Tis of Thee")

The tune for "America" was previously sung as the British national anthem, "God Save the Queen" (or King), in the eighteenth century. It has since been adapted as a patriotic song in the United States and in many other Anglophone nations. The words for "America" were written in 1831 by Samuel Francis Smith.

1. My coun - try, 'tis of thee, Sweet land of lib - er - ty,
2. My na - tive coun - try, thee, Land of the no - ble free,

Of thee I sing; Land where my fa - thers died, Land of the
Thy name I love; I love thy rocks and rills, Thy woods and

pil - grims' pride, From ev - ery moun - tain - side Let free - dom ring.
tem - pled hills; My heart with rap - ture thrills Like that a - bove.

"Chartres"

This tune, named for a town in France, is a French folk melody from the fifteenth century that was later harmonized by Charles Wood, a nineteenth-century English composer. The tune is most often sung to the words of the hymn "Saw You Never, in the Twilight," of which one verse is shown here. This hymn and those that follow are shown using traditional hymn notation: double bars at the end of each phrase indicate to the congregation where to breathe. Here, the measure at the end of the phrase is not complete until after the anacrusis for the following phrase, as reflected in the measure numbering.

"Old Hundredth"

This tune appeared in the Geneva Psalter, a collection of melodies that were used in Calvinist churches for singing texts from the book of Psalms. The name "Old Hundredth" indicates that this music was used to set Psalm 100. Both the melody and its harmonization are probably by Louis Bourgeois, a French composer who played an important role in gathering Calvinist hymns.

"Rosa Mystica"

"Rosa Mystica" is a German Christmas carol, better known in English as "Lo, How a Rose E'er Blooming." This version was harmonized in 1609 by Michael Praetorius, a composer and collector of Lutheran church music. No meter signature is provided because this hymn tune predates the current system of meter signatures: some measures imply $\frac{4}{4}$ and $\frac{3}{4}$ with a quarter-note beat unit; others $\frac{3}{2}$ or $\frac{2}{2}$ with a half-note beat unit.

"St. Anne"

The English composer William Croft wrote and harmonized this tune in 1708. Most often, it is sung as the hymn "O God Our Help in Ages Past" to words written by Isaac Watts in 1719, based on Psalm 90. The tune bears such a strong resemblance to the opening subject of Bach's Fugue in E♭ Major for organ (p. 38), composed in 1739, that Bach's work is now known as the "St. Anne" Fugue.

1. O God, our help in a - ges past, Our hope for years to come,
2. Be - fore the hills in or - der stood, Or earth re - ceived her frame,

Our shel - ter from the storm - y blast, And our e - ter - nal home:
From ev - er - last - ing thou art God, To end - less years the same.

"St. George's Windsor"

George J. Elvey, who was organist at St. George's Church in Windsor, England, composed this tune in 1858. Though it was originally written for the text "Hark, the Song of Jubilee," the music is now most frequently sung to the text "Come, Ye Thankful People, Come," adapted from a poem by Henry Alford, penned in 1844. In the United States, this hymn is typically sung at Thanksgiving.

Charles Ives (1874–1954)
"The Cage"

This song, published in 1922, is representative of the experimental style that Ives cultivated, which included dissonant and polytonal contexts for American folk and hymn tunes. The son of a Civil War bandleader, Ives spent his days as an insurance executive. His compositions, which were influenced by the sounds that he heard growing up in New England—and especially by his father's ideas about music—were rarely performed in his lifetime.

NOTE: All notes not marked with sharp or flat are natural.

Elisabeth-Claude Jacquet de la Guerre (1665–1729)
Gigue, from Suite No. 3 in A Minor

Elisabeth-Claude Jacquet de la Guerre was a composer and performer working primarily in Paris. She came from a family of musicians, played in the court of Louis XIV, and concertized widely. She is one of the few female composers of her day whose music has survived and is still performed. She composed an opera, numerous cantatas, chamber music, and several books of compositions for harpsichord, one of which includes this gigue. This work for harpsichord is notated with ornaments—symbols above the staff that tell performers to add embellishing notes to the notated pitch. When you listen, you will hear a more florid melodic line than the one notated here.

Scott Joplin (1868–1917)
"Pine Apple Rag"

Joplin's "Pine Apple Rag," named for the town Pine Apple, Alabama, was published in 1908.
Like all ragtime, this composition makes use of the "ragged rhythms," or syncopations,
that characterize the genre and are common to much African-American music written and
performed around the turn of the century.

Scott Joplin
"Solace"

"Solace," published in 1909, is not a typical rag, though it does make use of the syncopation that characterizes ragtime. It is sometimes listed with the subtitle "A Mexican Serenade," and it bears some resemblance to the tango. Like other Joplin compositions, "Solace" was made famous by its inclusion in the 1973 film *The Sting,* starring Paul Newman and Robert Redford.

Jerome Kern (1885–1945)

"Look for the Silver Lining"

Jerome Kern was a celebrated composer of songs for the musical theater and is best known for the musical *Show Boat*. Kern wrote over 700 songs; his hits include "Ol' Man River," "All the Things You Are," "A Fine Romance," and "Smoke Gets in Your Eyes." "Look for the Silver Lining" was first made popular in the musical *Sally* (1920), and was probably the inspiration for a memorable 1970s ad campaign for the International Ladies Garment Workers' Union ("Look for the union label, when you are buying a coat, dress, or blouse").

There's a way to make your ver - y big - gest troub - les small,
I am sure your point of view will ease the dai - ly grind,

Here's the hap - py se - cret of it all.
So I'll keep re - peat - ing in my mind.

Chorus

Look for the sil - ver lin - ing

p-f

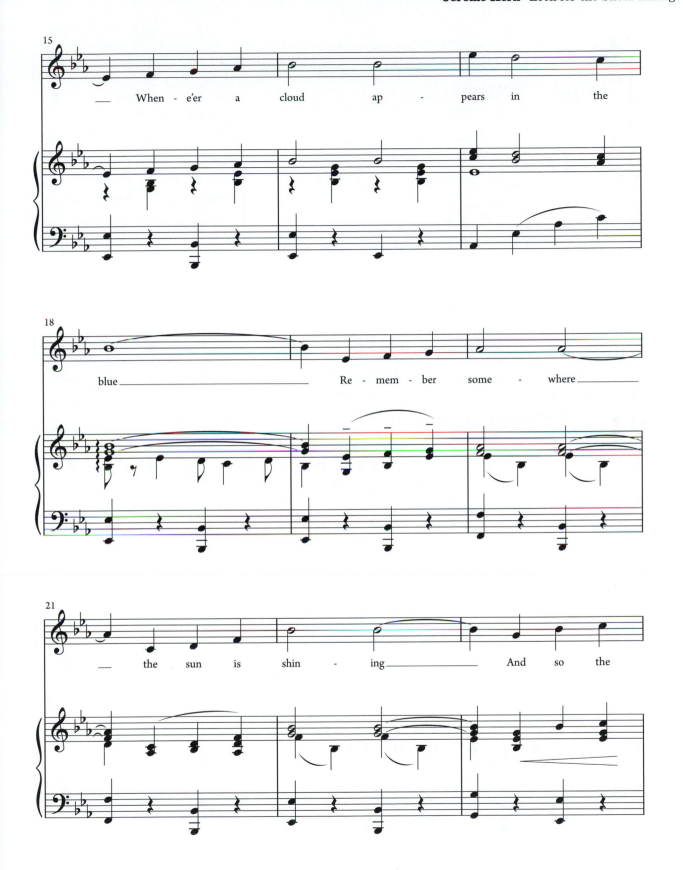

strife _____ So al - ways look for _____ the sil - ver

lin - ing _____ And try to find the sun - ny side of

1. life.

2. life. _____

Wolfgang Amadeus Mozart (1756–1791)

From *The Marriage of Figaro*: "Quanto duolmi, Susanna"
(recitative) and "Voi che sapete" (aria)

Mozart's opera *The Marriage of Figaro* received its premiere in 1786 in Vienna. Here, the
character Cherubino sings about his chronic love sickness. Though Cherubino is a male
character, Mozart wrote the music for a woman to sing; when a woman portrays a young man
on the operatic stage, her part is called a "pants role." In performances of this opera, cuts are
typically made to shorten its duration. Indications in the score show the cuts made in the
recording that accompanies this text.

Libretto by Lorenzo da Ponte

Cherubino

tar - ra, e l'ac-com-pa - gna. Io so - no sì tre - man - te...

Susanna

ma se Ma-da-ma vuo - le... Lo vuo - le, sì lo vuol: man-co pa - ro - le.

pro - vo, vi_____ ri - di - rò, è per me

nuo - vo, ca - pir nol so. Sen - to un af -

fet - to pien di de - sir, ch'o - ra è di -

-let - to, ch'o - ra mar - tir; ge - lo, e poi sen - to

per;   non tro-vo pa - ce not - te nè dì, ma pur mi pia - ce

lan - guir co - sì!   Voi, che sa - pe - te,

che co - sa è a - mor,   don - ne ve - de - te,

s'io l'ho nel cor,   don - ne ve - de - te,____

TEXT AND TRANSLATION

Countess:
Quanto duolmi, Susanna,
Che questo giovinetto abbia
Del Conte le stravaganze udite!
Ah! tu non sai ma per qual causa mai
Da me stessa ei non venne?
Dov' è la canzonetta?

How I grieve, Susanna,
That this young man has
Heard the extravagant stories of the count!
Ah, you don't know yet why he did not
See me himself in person?
Where is the love song?

Susanna:
Eccola,
Appunto facciam che ce la canti.
Zitto, vien gente, è desso;
Avanti, avanti, signor uffiziale!

Here it is,
As soon as he comes, we will have him sing it.
Quiet, someone's coming, it's him—
Come in, come in, mister officer!

Cherubino:
Ah, non chiamarmi con nome sì fatale!
Ei mi rammenta, che abbandonar
Degg'io comare tanto buona!
E tanto bella. Ah sì, certo!

Oh, do not call me with that fatal title!
And that reminds me that I must soon
Abandon my good lady!
And so beautiful. Ah yes, of course!

Susanna:
Ah sì, certo!
Ipocritone!
Via presto la canzone,
Che stamane a me deste,
A madama cantate.

Ah yes, of course!
Hypocrite!
Now quickly sing that love song
You gave me this morning,
Sing to Madame.

Countess:
Chi n'è l'autor?

Who is the author?

Susanna:
Guardate, egli ha due braci
Di rossor sulla faccia.

Look, he has two blushing embers
On his face.

Countess:
Prendi la mia chitarra, e l'accompagna.

Take my guitar and accompany him.

Cherubino:
Io sono sì tremante, ma se madama vuole—

I am trembling, but if Madame wishes—

Susanna:
Lo vuole, sì, lo vuol, manco parole.

She wishes, yes, she wishes—no more talk.

Cherubino:

Voi, che sapete che cosa è amor,	You who know what love is,
Donne, vedete s'io l'ho nel cor.	Ladies, see if I have it in my heart.
Quello ch'io provo vi ridirò,	What I feel I will recount to you,
è per me nuovo, capir nol so.	And for me it is new, I cannot understand it.
Sento un affetto pien di desir,	I feel an emotion, full of desire,
Ch'ora è diletto, ch'ora è martir.	Which now is pleasure, which now is suffering.
Gelo e poi sento l'alma avvampar,	I freeze and then I feel my soul burning up,
E in un momento torno a gelar.	And in a minute I am freezing again.
Ricerco un bene fuori di me,	I search for a good thing outside of me,
Non so chi'l tiene, non so cos'è.	I don't know how to take it; I don't know what it is.
Sospiro e gemo senza voler,	I sigh and moan without wanting to,
Palpito e tremor senza saper.	Throb and tremble without knowing why.
Non trovo pace notte nè dì,	I find no peace night or day,
Ma pur mi piace languir così.	Yet I enjoy languishing this way.
Voi, che sapete che cosa è amor,	You who know what love is,
Donne, vedete s'io l'ho nel cor.	Ladies, see if I have it in my heart.

Wolfgang Amadeus Mozart
Minuet in F Major, K. 2

This minuet, which Mozart wrote in 1762 when he was six years old, is typical of the small-scale keyboard works that make up many of the early compositions of this child prodigy. Mozart's composition appears in a notebook of piano pieces for his older sister, Maria Anna Mozart.

Wolfgang Amadeus Mozart
Minuet, from Sonata for Piano and Violin in C Major, K. 6

Mozart wrote this work—a piano sonata with violin accompaniment—when he was six or seven years old. Along with another violin sonata, it represents his first published work. Early in his life, Mozart toured European capitals as a child prodigy, performing on piano and violin—often with his sister Nannerl—for the nobility. The sonata was written during that tour, presumably for performance by the brother–sister duo.

Menuetto primo da Capo.

Wolfgang Amadeus Mozart
Piano Sonata in G Major, K. 283, first movement

Mozart composed this sonata in 1774 while in Munich for performances of his early opera *La finta giardiniera* (*The Pretend Garden-Maid*). It appears in his first published collection of piano sonatas. The recording that accompanies this anthology was made on a fortepiano, the type of instrument on which Mozart would have performed and for which he composed.

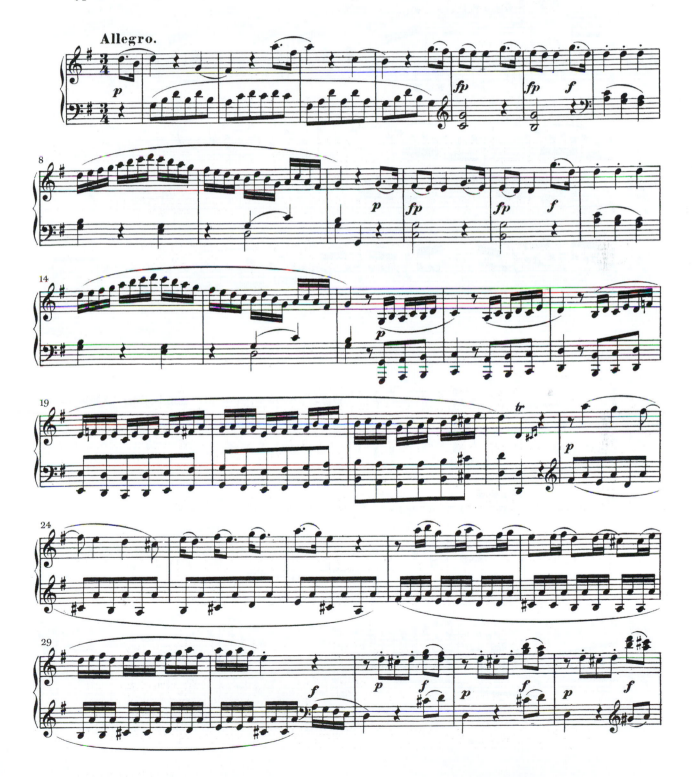

Wolfgang Amadeus Mozart
Piano Sonata in D Major, K. 284, third movement

This sonata was written in 1774 for the Baron von Dürnitz. The recording that accompanies this anthology was made on a fortepiano, which allows for striking changes in timbre and dynamic levels between variations.

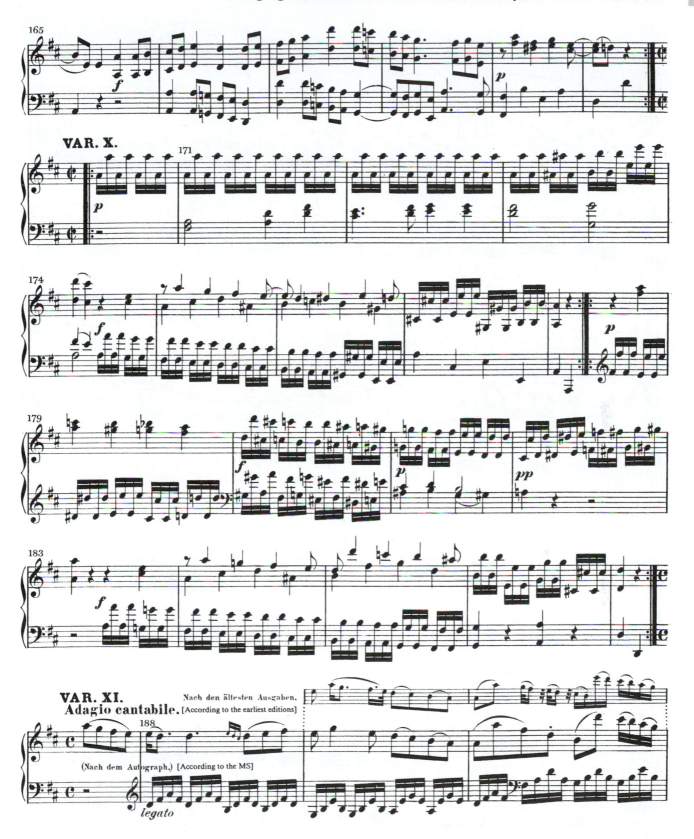

Wolfgang Amadeus Mozart
Piano Sonata in F Major, K. 332, first movement

This sonata was part of a collection of three piano sonatas that Mozart published in 1784. Unlike many earlier composers, Mozart frequently wrote for publication, rather than for aristocratic patrons. These works would have been purchased by amateur pianists for performance at home. The musical topics in this movement—such as the learned style and the hunt—would have been familiar to this audience.

Wolfgang Amadeus Mozart
Piano Sonata in C Major, K. 545

Mozart wrote this sonata in 1788 and characterized it as "for beginners." It was not published until 1805, after Mozart's death. Even today, this work is one of the first sonatas assigned to young pianists and is one of his works best known by amateur performers. All three movements are included on the recordings, in two performances: on fortepiano and on a modern piano, for comparison.

Wolfgang Amadeus Mozart
From *Requiem*: Kyrie eleison and Dies irae

The Kyrie and Dies irae are the second and third movements from Mozart's *Requiem,* a mass
for a Catholic funeral service. Written in 1791, the mass was left unfinished at his death, and
was completed by Franz Xavier Süssmayer, a Viennese composer who may have studied with
Mozart. In the film adaptation of Peter Shaffer's play *Amadeus,* the *Requiem* is famously (and
fictionally) completed by Mozart's rival Antonio Salieri, from themes sung to him by Mozart on
his deathbed.

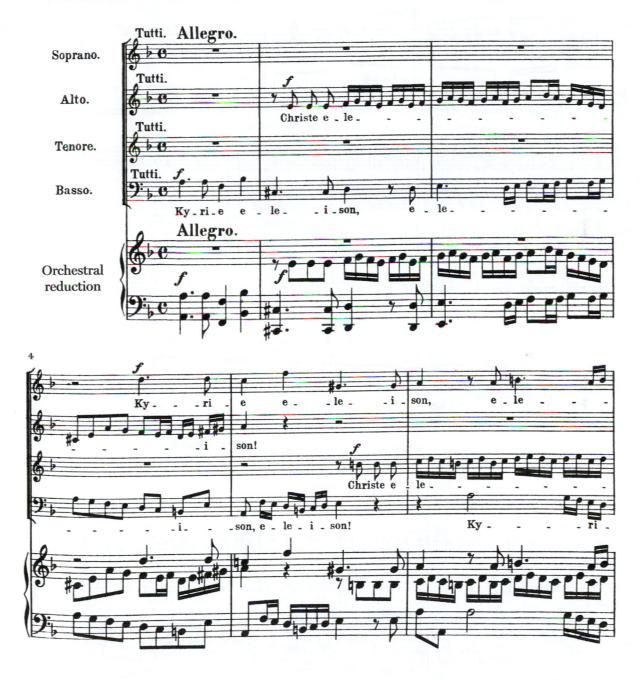

TEXT AND TRANSLATION

Kyrie eleison

Kyrie eleison,
Kyrie eleison,
Christe eleison.

Dies irae

Dies ire, dies illa,
solvet saeclum in favilla,
teste David cum Sybilla.

Quantus tremor est futurus,
Judex est venturus,
Cuncta stricte discussurus.

Lord, Have Mercy

Lord, have mercy,
Christ, have mercy,
Lord, have mercy.

Day of Wrath

Day of wrath, a day when
The world will dissolve in ashes,
As foretold by David and the Sibyl.

What trembling there will be
When the judge comes
To adjudicate all things strictly.

Wolfgang Amadeus Mozart
String Quartet in D Minor, K. 421, first and third movements

This quartet, composed in 1783, is part of a set of six quartets that Mozart published together and dedicated to Haydn. During Mozart's lifetime, Haydn's quartets were widely admired; in his "Haydn Quartets," Mozart takes inspiration from the older composer. (For an example of a Haydn quartet movement, see p. 241.)

Menuetto D.C.

Wolfgang Amadeus Mozart
Variations on "Ah, vous dirai-je Maman"

Mozart composed this theme and variations early in the 1780s. The theme is a French folk song, "Ah, vous dirai-je Maman," the same tune as "Twinkle, Twinkle, Little Star." Because this tune is so familiar, it makes this sectional variation set an ideal vehicle for studying variation technique.

Krzysztof Penderecki (b. 1933)

Threnody for the Victims of Hiroshima

(to rehearsal 25)

Composed in 1960, the *Threnody*, with its evocative title and striking sonic character, brought Polish composer Krzysztof Penderecki international recognition. The piece is significant for its graphic notation, invented by Penderecki and employed in many of his later compositions. Though he initially gave it a generic title, after hearing a performance of the work, Penderecki renamed it to memorialize the victims of the world's first atomic bomb.

ABBREVIATIONS AND SYMBOLS

Sharpen a quarter-tone.

Sharpen three quarter-tones.

Flatten a quarter-tone.

Flatten three quarter-tones.

Highest note of the instrument (no definite pitch).

Play between bridge and tailpiece.

Arpeggio on 4 strings behind the bridge.

Play on the tailpiece (arco) by bowing the tailpiece at an angle of 90° to its longer axis.

Molto vibrato.

Very slow vibrato with a ¼ tone frequency difference produced by sliding the finger.

Very rapid non-rhythmisized tremolo.

ordinario	ord.
sul ponticello	s. p.
sul tasto	s. t.
col legno	c. l.
legno battuto	l. batt.

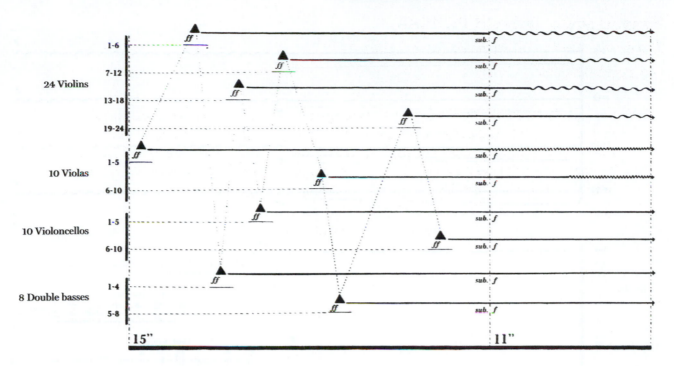

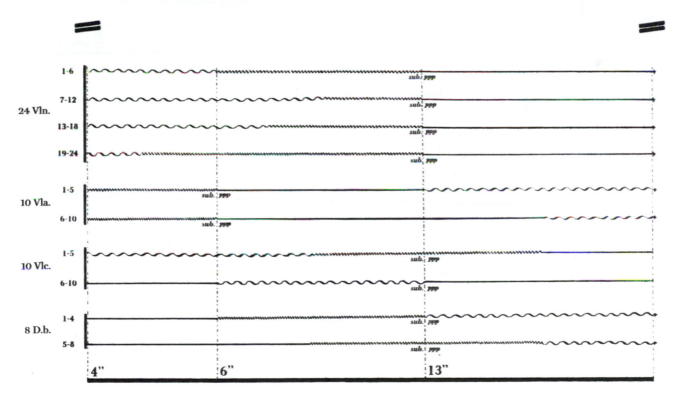

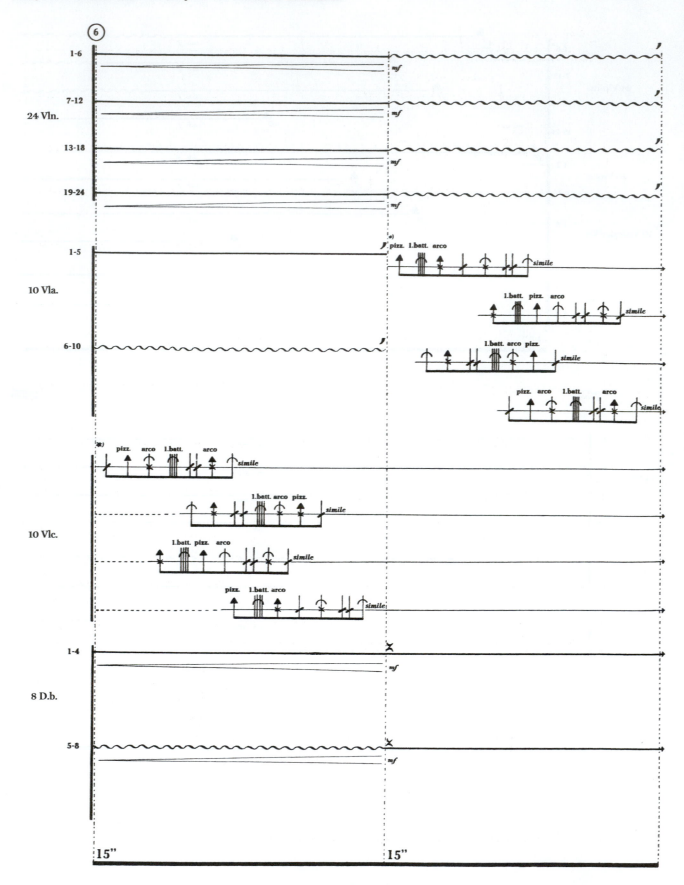

*Each instrumentalist chooses one of the four given groups and executes it (within a fixed space of time) as rapidly as possible.

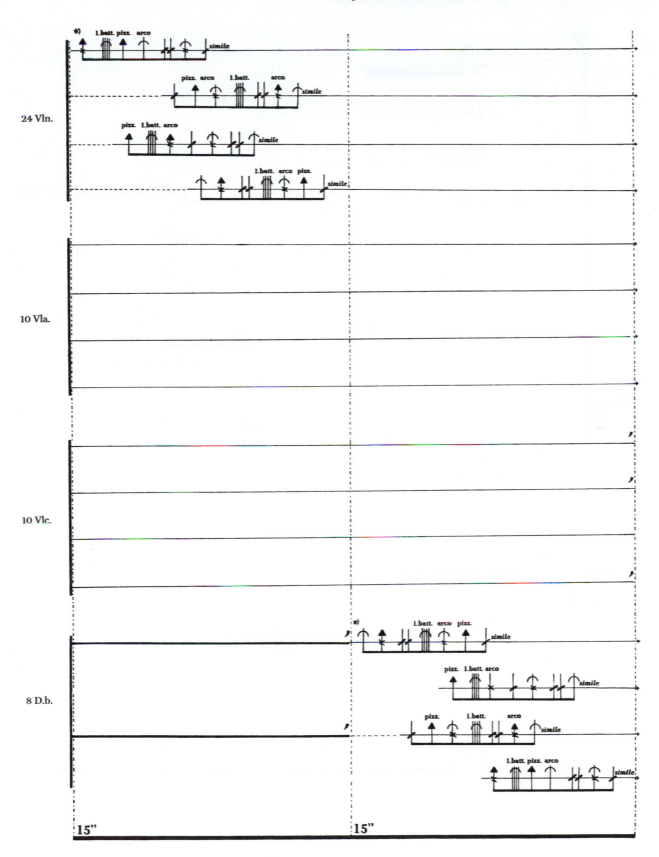

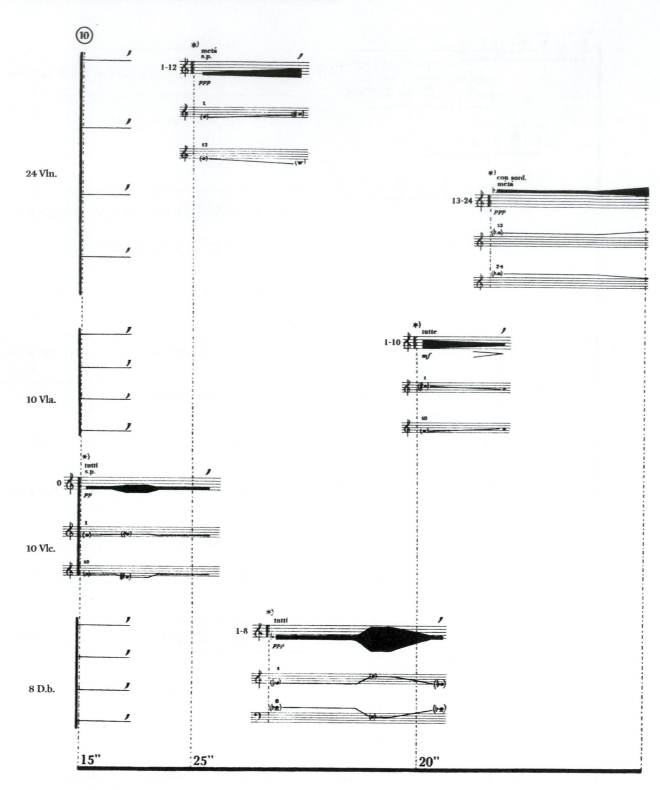

*Exact notation is given in the parts.

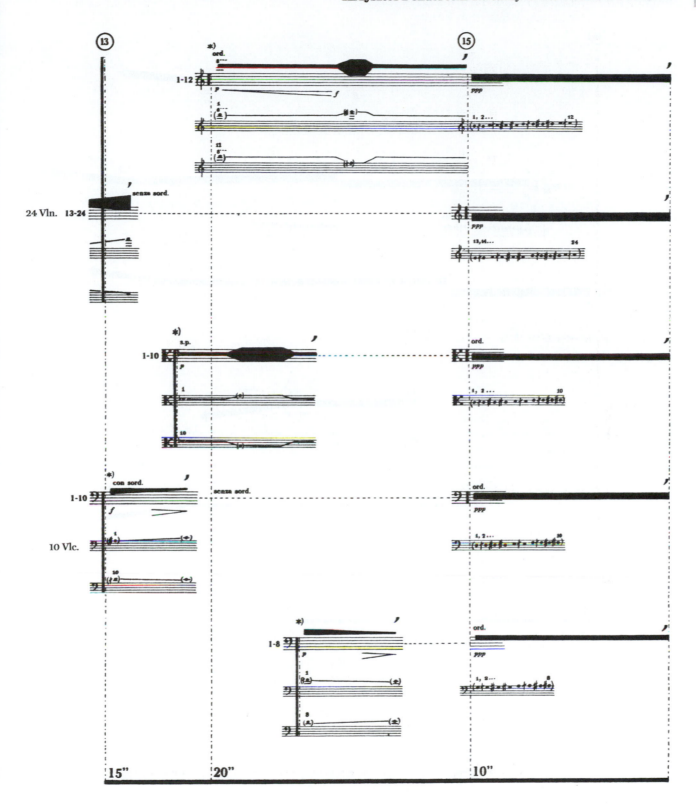

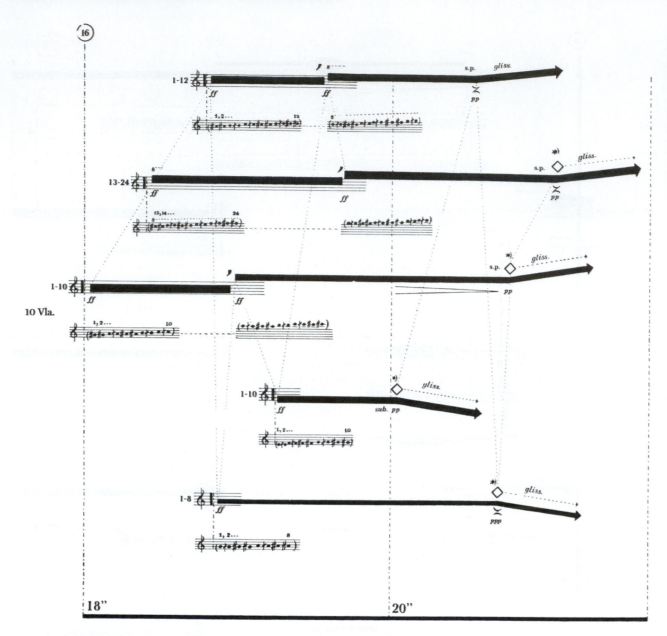

*Flageolet tones.

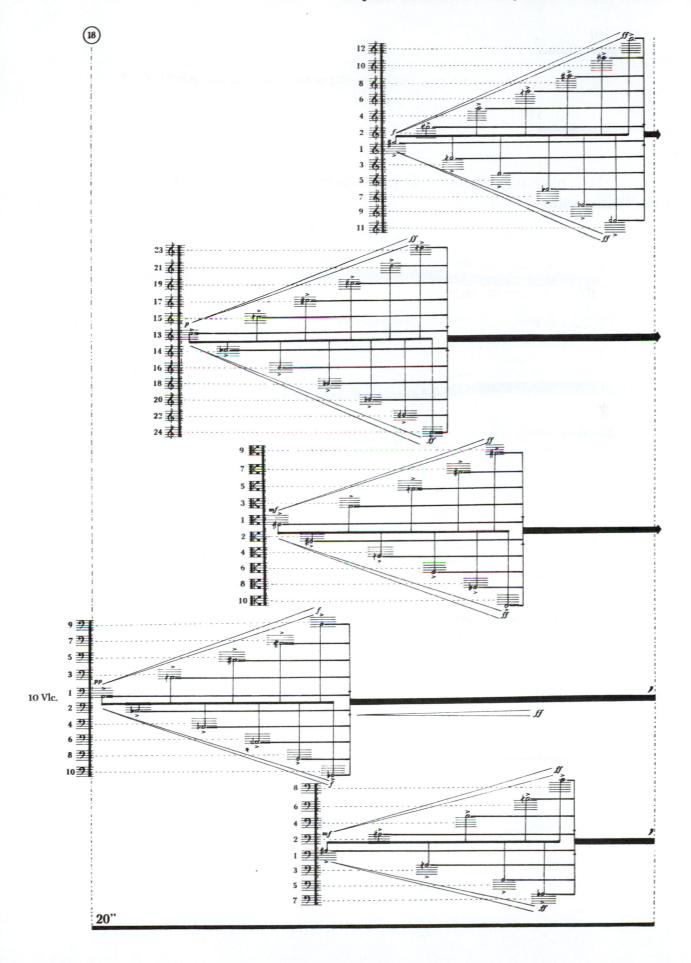

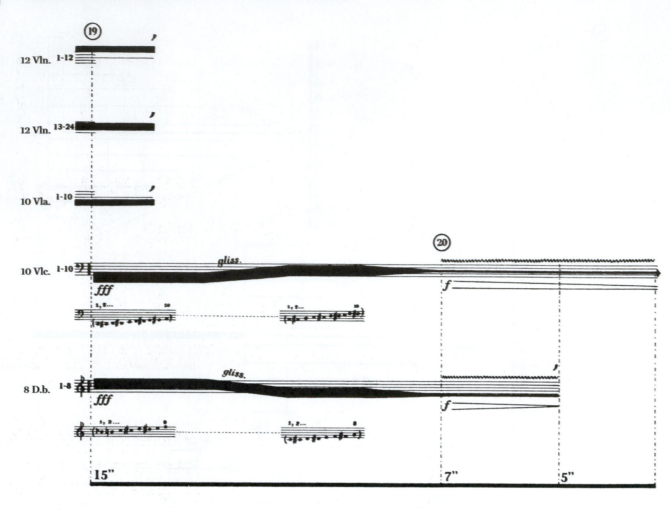

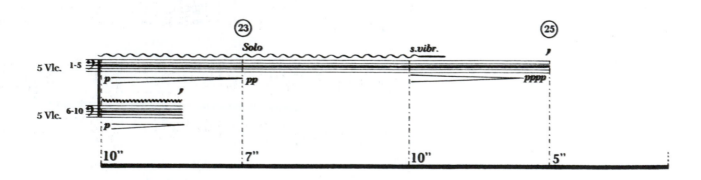

Henry Purcell (1659–1695)
From *Dido and Aeneas*

Dido and Aeneas, composed in 1689, is based on a passage from Virgil's *Aeneid.* In the opera, the Trojan prince, Aeneas, and Dido, queen of Carthage, fall in love; yet a sorceress tricks Aeneas into abandoning Dido, leading to her demise. In "Ah, Belinda, I am prest," the first aria of the opera, Dido reflects on her initial anguish at being pursued by Aeneas. In "When I am laid in earth," Dido, heartbroken at her abandonment by Aeneas, prepares for death. Both arias are written above a ground bass.

"Ah, Belinda, I am prest" (aria)

Libretto by Nahum Tate

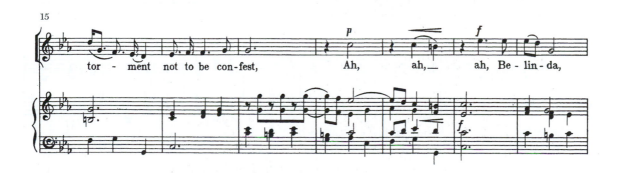

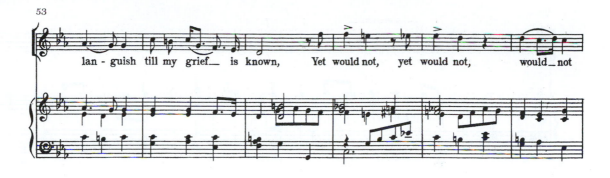

"Thy hand, Belinda" (recitative) and
"When I am laid in earth" (aria)

-vades me   Death   is   now   a   wel - come   guest.

When I   am   laid,   am   laid _____ in

earth, may my   wrongs___   cre - ate   no   trou - ble, no   trou-ble in__ thy

breast.   When I am   laid,   am   laid_____ in earth, may my

wrongs cre-ate no trou-ble, no trouble in __ thy breast.   Re-

-mem-ber me,   re-mem-ber me,   But ah! _____ forget my

fate, Re-member me,   but ah! _____   for-get my fate Re-

-member me,   re-member me,   But ah! _____   forget my

fate, Re - mem-ber me, but ah! _____ for - get my fate!

Henry Purcell
"Music for a While"

Purcell wrote "Music for a While" in 1692, as part of the incidental music to be performed for John Dryden and Nathaniel Lee's English adaptation of the ancient Greek tragedy *Oedipus Rex.* Many of Purcell's works were originally composed for the theater. The text refers to Alecto, one of the Furies, who were often depicted with wings and with their heads wreathed with serpents. This score shows an unfigured bass; in performance, the continuo player would fill in the harmonies at the keyboard.

Maurice Ravel (1875–1937)

"Aoua!," from *Chansons madécasses*, for soprano, flute, cello, and piano

"Aoua!" is one of three songs that comprise the *Chansons madécasses* (*Songs of Madagascar*), composed in 1925–26 for Elizabeth Sprague Coolidge, an American pianist and patron of chamber music. Ravel's songs are settings of poems about the island of Madagascar by Évariste de Parny, and "Aoua!" describes the fates of European colonists who attempted to enslave the Madagascans. The song poignantly mixes the languid exoticism of the foreign locale with the stirring cries of an oppressed people.

Text by Évariste de Parny

Les blancs pro _ mirent, et ce _ pendant ils fai _

_saient des retranchemens. Un fort me _ na _ çant s'é _ le _ va; le tonner _ re fut renfermé

dans des bouches d'airain; leurs prê _ tres vou _ lu _ rent nous don _ ner un Dieu____

que nous ne connaissons pas; _____ ils par_lè _ rent en _ fin d'o_bé_is_san_ce et d'escla_

FLAUTO

_va _ _ _ ge: plu_tôt la mort! _____ Le car _ na _ ge fut long et ter_

_ri _ ble; mais, mal_gré la fou_dre qu'ils vo_mis_saient, et qui é_cra_sait des armées en_

tières, ils furent tous extermi . nés. Aoua!_____ Aoua!_____

Allegro feroce

Mé . fi . ez-vous des blancs!

Nous a . vons vu de nouveaux ty . rans, plus forts et plus nom . breux,___ plan .

47

ter leur pa_vil_lon sur__ le ri_va_ge: le

51

ciel   a com_bat_tu pour__nous; il a fait tom _ ber sur__eux

55

les__pluies, les tem _ pê_tes et les vents em _ poi_sonnés.____

TEXT AND TRANSLATION

"Aoua!"

Aoua! Aoua! Méfiez-vous des blancs,
Habitants du rivage.
Du temps de nos pères,
Des blancs descendirent dans cette île.
On leur dit: Voilà des terres,
Que vos femmes les cultivent.
Soyez justes, soyez bons,
Et devenez nos frères.

Les blancs promirent, et cependant
Ils faisaient des retranchements.
Un fort menaçant s'éleva;
Le tonnerre fut renfermé
Dans des bouches d'airain;
Leurs prêtres voulurent nous donner
Un Dieu que nous ne connaissons pas,
Ils parlèrent enfin
D'obéissance et d'esclavage.

Plutôt la mort!
Le carnage fut long et terrible;
Mais, malgré la foudre qu'ils vormissaient,
Et qui écrasait des armées entières,
Ils furent tous exterminés.

Aoua! Aoua! Méfiez-vous des blancs!

Nous avons vu de nouveaux tyrans,
Plus forts et plus nombreaux,
Planter leur pavillon sur le rivage:
Le ciel a combattu pour nous;
Il a fait tomber sur eux les pluies,
Les tempêtes et les vents empoisonnés.
Ils ne sont plus, et nous vivons,
Et nous vivons libres.

Aoua! Méfiez-vous des blancs,
Habitants du rivage.

"Aoua!"

Aoua! Aoua! Beware of the white men,
Inhabitants of the shore.
In the times of our fathers,
The white men descended to this island.
They said to them: "Here is some land
That your women may cultivate.
Be fair, be good,
And become our brothers."

The white men promised, and yet
They were making entrenchments.
A menacing fort rose up,
The thunder was confined
In the mouths of cannons.
Their priests wanted to give us
A God that we did not know.
Finally, they spoke
Of obedience and slavery.

Rather death!
The carnage was long and terrible,
But despite the lightning that they vomited,
Which crushed entire armies,
They were all exterminated.

Aoua! Aoua! Beware of the white men!

We saw new tyrants,
Stronger and more numerous,
Planting their flag on the shore.
Heaven fought for us;
It made rain fall on them,
Storms and poisoned winds.
They are no more, and we live,
And we live free.

Aoua! Aoua! Beware of the white men,
Inhabitants of the shore.

Maurice Ravel

Pavane pour une infante défunte

Ravel wrote this work in 1899, when he was a student at the Paris Conservatory, and later orchestrated it. A pavane is a slow Spanish dance that was popular in Europe during the Baroque era. The title, often translated "Pavane for a Dead Princess," does not refer to a specific princess, but rather to the courtly culture in which such a dance flourished. Comparing the original with its 1910 orchestration can provide the pianist with important clues as to the composer's intended mood, articulation, and color.

Steve Reich (b. 1936)

Piano Phase (patterns 1–32)

Reich composed *Piano Phase* in 1967. Like many of his early works, the composition received its premiere at an art gallery: the Park Place Gallery in New York, known for sponsoring performances of modern music. Because of its extended repetition of a simple melodic idea, *Piano Phase* is an example of the artistic movement that came to be known as minimalism. In this work, the two pianos begin together, then Piano II accelerates until it is one sixteenth note ahead. Listen for the pianos to move out of phase, then lock in on the new alignment of the patterns.

The piece may be played an octave lower than written, when played on marimbas.

a.v.s. = accelerando very slightly.

1967

Arnold Schoenberg (1874–1951)
Drei Klavierstücke, Op. 11, No. 1

This work, part of a collection of three piano pieces that Schoenberg wrote in 1909, is often regarded as his first fully atonal composition. In his writings, Schoenberg described a process he called "developing variation," where a small number of motives are constantly developed through the course of a composition. That process played a major role in early atonal compositions such as this one. One listening strategy is to follow the opening melody in its various transformations—both melodic and harmonic—throughout the movement.

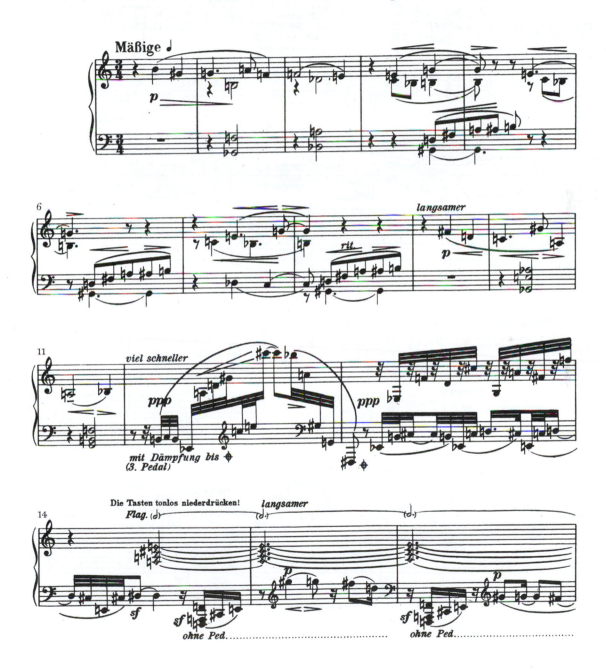

Arnold Schoenberg

Klavierstück, Op. 33a

Schoenberg composed this *Klavierstück* in 1929 for an anthology of twentieth-century piano music published by Universal Edition. The piece exemplifies Schoenberg's use of serialism, a compositional technique he developed in the 1920s, while retaining some aspects of sonata form.

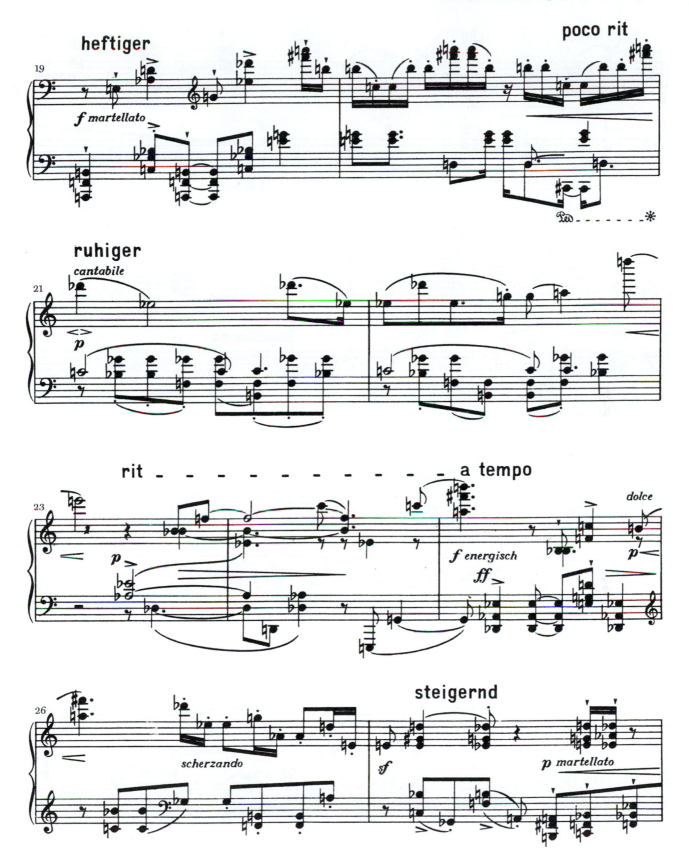

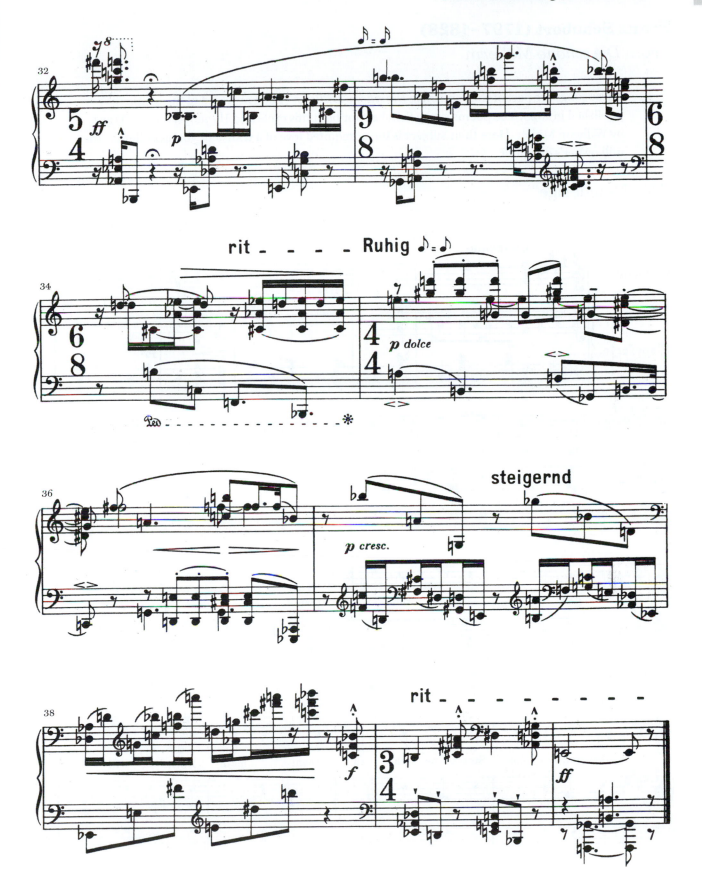

Franz Schubert (1797–1828)
From *Die schöne Müllerin*

These songs are part of the song cycle *Die schöne Müllerin* (The Fair Maid of the Mill), published in 1823. The poems set by Schubert for both this cycle and *Winterreise* (p. 421) are by Wilhelm Müller. Here their subject is the unrequited love of a transient young miller for the mill owner's daughter.

"Der Neugierige"

Text by Wilhelm Müller

TEXT AND TRANSLATION

"Der Neugierige"

Ich frage keine Blume,
Ich frage keinen Stern,
Sie können mir alle nicht sagen,
Was ich erführ' so gern.

Ich bin ja auch kein Gärtner,
Die Sterne steh'n zu hoch;
Mein Bächlein will ich fragen,
Ob mich mein Herz belog.

O Bächlein meiner Liebe,
Wie bist du heut' so stumm!
Will ja nur Eines wissen,
Ein Wörtchen um und um.

Ja, heißt das eine Wörtchen,
Das andre heißet Nein,
Die beiden Wörtchen
Schließen die ganze Welt mir ein.

O Bächlein meiner Liebe,
Was bist du wunderlich!
Will's ja nicht weiter sagen,
Sag' Bächlein, liebt sie mich?

"The Inquisitive One"

I ask no flower,
I ask no star,
They cannot tell me,
What I want to know so much.

I am, anyway, no gardener,
The stars are up too high,
My brooklet I will ask
Whether my heart deceived me.

O brooklet of my love,
Why are you today so silent!
I want to know only one thing,
One little word over and over.

"Yes" is the one little word,
The other is "No";
These two little words
Comprise the whole world to me.

O brooklet of my love,
How strange you are!
I will not repeat it,
Speak, brooklet, does she love me?

"Morgengruß"

Text by Wilhelm Müller

TEXT AND TRANSLATION

"Morgengruß"

Guten Morgen, schöne Müllerin!
Wo steckst du gleich das Köpfchen hin,
Als wär' dir was geschehen?
Verdrießt dich denn mein Gruß so schwer?
Verstört dich denn mein Blick so sehr?
So muß ich wieder gehen.

O laß mich nur von ferne steh'n,
Nach deinem lieben Fenster seh'n,
Von ferne, ganz von ferne!
Du blondes Köpfchen, komm hervor!
Hervor aus eurem runden Tor,
Ihr blauen Morgensterne!

Ihr schlummertrunk'nen Äugelein,
Ihr taubetrübten Blümelein,
Was scheuet ihr die Sonne?
Hat es die Nacht so gut gemeint,
Daß ihr euch schließt und bückt und weint
Nach ihrer stillen Wonne?

Nun schüttelt ab der Träume Flor,
Und hebt euch frisch und frei empor
In Gottes hellen Morgen!
Die Lerche wirbelt in der Luft,
Und aus dem tiefen Herzen ruft
Die Liebe Leid und Sorgen.

"Morning Greeting"

Good morning, beautiful millermaid!
Why did you immediately hide your little head
As if something had happened to you?
Does my greeting irritate you so much?
Does my gaze upset you so much?
Then I must go again.

Oh let me just stand from afar,
Looking at your dear window,
From afar, completely from afar!
You little blond head, come out!
Out from your round gate,
You blue morning stars!

You slumber-drunk little eyes,
You dew-saddened little flowers,
Why do you shun the sun?
Has the night been so good to you
That you close up and bend over and cry
For its quiet bliss?

Now shake off the veil of dreams
And rise up fresh and free
In God's bright morning!
The skylark warbles in the air;
And from the depths of the heart calls
The pain of love and worry.

Franz Schubert
"Du bist die Ruh"

"Du bist die Ruh," composed in 1823, is a setting of a poem by Frederich Rückert. Schubert was not the only composer inspired by this poem; Fanny Hensel also set it. (For other works by Fanny Hensel, see pp. 245–254.)

Text by Frederich Rückert

mein Aug' und Herz.

Kehr' ein bei mir, und schlie - sse du still hin - ter

dir die Pfor - ten zu. Treib' an - dern Schmerz aus die - ser

Brust! Voll sei dies Herz von dei - ner Lust, von dei - ner

Lust.

TEXT AND TRANSLATION

Du bist die Ruh,	You are rest,
Der Friede mild,	The gentle peace,
Die Sehnsucht du	You are the yearning
Und was sie stillt.	And what satiates it.
Ich weihe dir	I consecrate to you,
Voll Lust und Schmerz	Full of joy and pain,
Zur Wohnung hier	As a dwelling here
Mein Aug' und Herz.	My eyes and heart.
Kehr' ein bei mir,	Come live with me,
Und schließe du	And close
Still hinter dir	The gates
Die Pforten zu.	Quietly behind you.
Treib' andern Schmerz	Drive other pain
Aus dieser Brust!	From this breast!
Voll sei dies Herz	May this heart be full
Von deiner Lust.	Of your joy.
Dies Augenzelt	The tabernacle of my eyes
Von deinem Glanz	From your splendor
Allein erhellt,	Alone is illuminated,
O füll' es ganz!	Oh fill it completely!

Franz Schubert
"Erlkönig"

Schubert composed this song in 1815, when he was only eighteen years old. Goethe's poem, the text for this song, borrows the Elf King (Erlkönig) from Scandinavian mythology, where the Elf King is a spirit who haunts forests. Travelers with the misfortune of seeing or being touched by this spirit meet their death. This poem was set by many composers (including Schubert's contemporaries Carl Loewe and Johann Friedrich Reichardt), but Schubert's setting is by far the best known.

Text by Johann Wolfgang von Goethe

TEXT AND TRANSLATION

"Erlkönig"

Wer reitet so spät durch Nacht und Wind?
Es ist der Vater mit seinem Kind;
Er hat den Knaben wohl in dem Arm,
Er faßt ihn sicher, er hält ihn warm.

"Mein Sohn, was birgst du so bang dein Gesicht?"
"Siehst, Vater, du den Erlkönig nicht?
Den Erlenkönig mit Kron' und Schweif?"
"Mein Sohn, es ist ein Nebelstreif."

"Du liebes Kind, komm, geh mit mir!
Gar schöne Spiele spiel ich mit dir;
Manch bunte Blumen sind an dem Strand,
Meine Mutter hat manch' gülden Gewand."

"Mein Vater, mein Vater, und hörest du nicht,
Was Erlenkönig mir leise verspricht?"
"Sei ruhig, bleibe ruhig, mein Kind;
In dürren Blättern säuselt der Wind."

"Willst, feiner Knabe, du mit mir gehn?
Meine Töchter sollen dich warten schön;
Meine Töchter führen den nächtlichen Reihn
Und wiegen und tanzen und singen dich ein."

"Mein Vater, mein Vater, und siehst du nicht dort
Erlkönigs Töchter am düstern Ort?"
"Mein Sohn, mein Sohn, ich seh es genau:
Es scheinen die alten Weiden so grau."

"Ich liebe dich, mich reizt deine schöne Gestalt;
Und bist du nicht willig, so brauch' ich Gewalt."
"Mein Vater, mein Vater, jetzt faßt er mich an!
Erlkönig hat mir ein Leids getan!"

Dem Vater grauset's, er reitet geschwind,
Er hält in Armen das ächzende Kind,
Erreicht den Hof mit Müh' und Not:
In seinen Armen das Kind war tot.

"The Elf King"

Who rides so late through night and wind?
It is the father with his child.
He has the boy secure in his arm;
He holds him safe, he keeps him warm.

"My son, why do you hide your face, so afraid?"
"Father, do you not see the Elf King?
The Elf King with crown and train?"
"My son, it is a strip of mist."

"You dear child, come away with me!
Wonderful games I will play with you;
Many colorful flowers are on the shore,
My mother has many golden garments."

"My father, my father, don't you hear
What the Elf King is quietly promising me?"
"Be still, stay calm, my child:
The wind whispers in dry leaves."

"Will you, fine boy, come with me?
My daughters shall attend to you well.
My daughters will lead their nightly round dance
And rock you and dance with you and sing to you."

"My father, my father, don't you see there
The Elf King's daughters in that dark place?"
"My son, my son, I see it clearly enough:
The old willows shine so gray."

"I love you, I am tempted by your beautiful form;
And if you are not willing, I will use force."
"My father, my father, now he has grabbed me!
The Elf King has hurt me!"

The father shudders, he rides quickly.
He holds in his arms the moaning child.
He reaches the courtyard with effort and distress;
In his arms the child was dead.

Franz Schubert

From *Moments musicaux*, Op. 94: No. 6, in A♭ Major

In 1828, Schubert included this *Moment musical* in a collection of six brief piano pieces, together called *Moments musicaux*. Along with the Impromptus, these are among the most frequently performed of Schubert's short piano works.

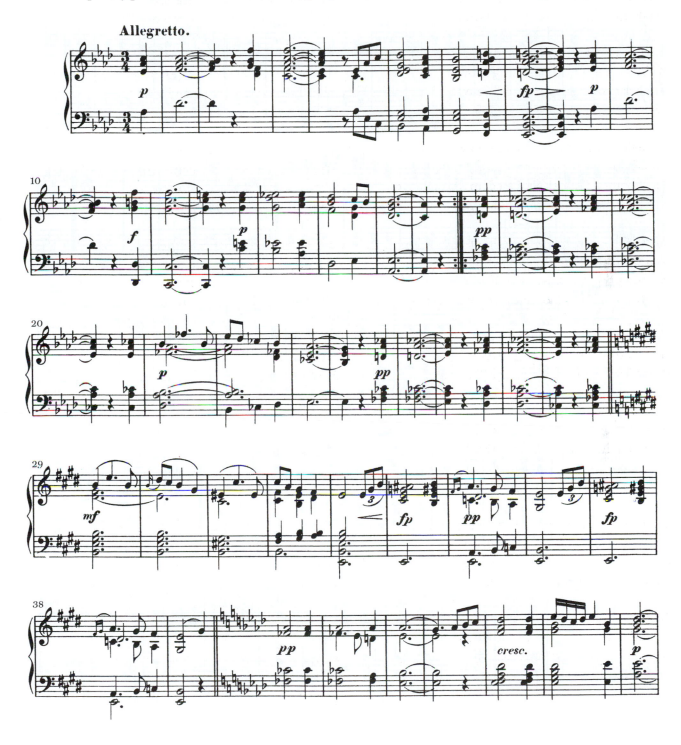

Allegretto D.C.

Franz Schubert
Waltz in B Minor, Op. 18, No. 6

The waltz is a German dance in triple meter that enjoyed great popularity in the nineteenth century. This one belongs to a set of dance pieces Schubert composed in 1815. At parties, Schubert frequently improvised short piano waltzes, like this one, for dancing.

Franz Schubert

"Der Lindenbaum," from *Winterreise*

Schubert published *Winterreise,* a cycle of songs to texts by Wilhelm Müller, in 1828. Within a song cycle, a collection of songs set to the words of a single poet or poems on a general theme, the progression of individual songs may tell a story. *Winterreise* tells the story of a spurned lover who undertakes a journey in an attempt to find peace; in "Der Lindenbaum," a Linden tree evokes the lover's memories of a happy past while also hinting at an unhappy future.

Text by Wilhelm Müller

TEXT AND TRANSLATION

"Der Lindenbaum," from *Winterreise*

Am Brunnen vor dem Tore
Da steht ein Lindenbaum;
Ich träumt' in seinem Schatten
So manchen süßen Traum.

Ich schnitt in seine Rinde
So manches liebe Wort;
Es zog in Freud' und Leide
Zu ihm mich immer fort.

Ich mußt' auch heute wandern
Vorbei in tiefer Nacht,
Da hab' ich noch im Dunkel
Die Augen zugemacht.

Und seine Zweige rauschten,
Als riefen sie mir zu:
Komm her zu mir, Geselle,
Hier find'st du deine Ruh'!

Die kalten Winde bliesen
Mir grad' ins Angesicht;
Der Hut flog mir vom Kopfe,
Ich wendete mich nicht.

Nun bin ich manche Stunde
Entfernt von jenem Ort,
Und immer hör' ich's rauschen:
Du fändest Ruhe dort!

"The Linden Tree," from *Winter Journey*

At the well in front of the gate
There stands a linden tree.
I have dreamed in its shadows
So many sweet dreams.

I carved in its bark
So many loving words;
It drew me, in joy and sorrow,
To itself always.

I had to travel by it again today
In dead of night,
I had, even in the darkness,
To close my eyes.

And its branches rustled
As if calling to me:
"Come here to me, traveler,
Here you will find your peace!"

The cold wind blew
Directly in my face,
The hat flew off my head,
I did not turn back.

Now I am many hours
Away from that place,
And still I hear the rustling:
"There you would have found peace."

Clara Schumann (1819–1896)
"Liebst du um Schönheit"

"Liebst du um Schönheit" ("If You Love for Beauty") was published in 1841 as part of a collection of songs composed by Clara Schumann and her husband, Robert, all with texts by Friedrich Rückert. The Schumanns frequently collaborated on song composition, reading texts to one another and playing each other's music at the piano.

Text by Friedrich Rückert

TEXT AND TRANSLATION

Liebst du um Schönheit,	If you love for beauty,
O nicht mich liebe!	Oh do not love me!
Liebe die Sonne,	Love the sun;
Sie trägt ein gold'nes Haar!	She has golden hair!
Liebst du um Jugend,	If you love for youthfulness,
O nicht mich liebe!	Oh do not love me!
Liebe den Frühling,	Love the springtime;
Der jung ist jedes Jahr!	It is young every year!
Liebst du um Schätze,	If you love for wealth,
O nicht mich liebe.	Oh do not love me!
Liebe die Meerfrau,	Love the mermaid;
sie hat viel Perlen klar.	She has many fair pearls.
Liebst du um Liebe,	If you love for love itself,
O ja, mich liebe!	Oh yes, love me!
Liebe mich immer,	Love me always,
Dich lieb' ich immerdar!	And I will love you forever!

Clara Schumann
Romanze, Op. 21, No. 1

This work, published in 1855, is an example of a character piece. Popularized by nineteenth-century composers, character pieces are short works focused on a single extramusical idea, typically with a colorful, evocative title. They were often performed in salons, small intimate gatherings of friends that featured performances of music. Also in the anthology are character pieces by Clara's husband Robert Schumann, with titles that translate as "Humming Song," "Wild Rider," and "Little Folk Song."

Robert Schumann (1810–1856)

From *Album for the Young*, Op. 68

Schumann completed his *Album for the Young*, a collection of pedagogical piano pieces, in 1848. Several of the pieces were originally written for Clara and Robert Schumann's daughter Marie. Like the three that appear here, most of the compositions in the album have descriptive titles and are short character pieces that depict the "story" of their titles.

No. 3: "Trällerliedchen" ("Humming Song")

No. 8: "Wilder Reiter" ("Wild Rider")

No. 9: "Volksliedchen" ("Little Folk Song")

Robert Schumann

From *Dichterliebe*

Schumann was known for focusing his compositional energies exclusively on a single genre, such as the song or the symphony, for an extended period of time. He composed *Dichterliebe*, a song cycle to texts of Heinrich Heine, during what he called his "year of song," 1840. Over the course of this year, Schumann composed more than 160 art songs, while he waged a legal battle against his future wife's father, who had refused to allow their marriage.

"Im wunderschönen Monat Mai"

Text by Heinrich Heine

TEXT AND TRANSLATION

"Im wunderschönen Monat Mai," from *Dichterliebe*

Im wunderschönen Monat Mai,
Als alle Knospen sprangen,
Da ist in meinem Herzen
Die Liebe aufgegangen.

Im wunderschönen Monat Mai,
Als alle Vögel sangen,
Da hab' ich ihr gestanden
Mein Sehnen und Verlangen.

"In the Lovely Month of May," from *The Poet's Love*

In the lovely month of May,
When all the buds were bursting,
Then within my heart
Love began to blossom.

In the lovely month of May,
When all the birds were singing,
Then I confessed to her
My longing and desire.

"Ich grolle nicht"

Text by Heinrich Heine

TEXT AND TRANSLATION

"Ich grolle nicht," from *Dichterliebe*

Ich grolle nicht, und wenn das Herz auch bricht.
Ewig verlor'nes Lieb! Ich grolle nicht.
Wie du auch strahlst in Diamantenpracht,
Es fällt kein Strahl in deines Herzens Nacht.
Das weiß ich längst.

Ich grolle nicht, und wenn das Herz auch bricht.
Ich sah dich ja im Traume,
Und sah die Nacht in deines Herzens Raume,
Und sah die Schlang', die dir am Herzen frißt,
Ich sah, mein Lieb, wie sehr du elend bist.
Ich grolle nicht.

"I Bear No Grudge," from *The Poet's Love*

I bear no grudge, even if my heart breaks.
Eternally lost Love! I bear no grudge.
Even as you beam in diamond splendor,
There falls no beam into your heart's night.
That I have known for a long time.

I bear no grudge, even if my heart breaks.
I saw you in a dream,
And saw the night in the space of your heart,
And saw the snake that devours your heart;
I saw, my love, how much you are miserable.
I bear no grudge.

Robert Schumann

"Widmung," from *Myrthen*

Like *Dichterliebe* (p. 437), the collection of songs in *Myrthen* was composed during Schumann's memorable song year, 1840. Schumann presented these songs, composed to texts by a variety of poets, to Clara as a wedding gift.

Text by Friedrich Rückert

TEXT AND TRANSLATION

"Widmung," from *Myrthen*

Du meine Seele, du mein Herz,
Du meine Wonn', o du mein Schmerz,
Du meine Welt, in der ich lebe,
Mein Himmel du, darein ich schwebe,
O du mein Grab, in das hinab
Ich ewig meinen Kummer gab.

Du bist die Ruh, du bist der Frieden,
Du bist der Himmel mir beschieden.
Daß du mich liebst, macht mich mir werth,
Dein Blick hat mich vor mir verklärt,
Du hebst mich liebend über mich,
Mein guter Geist, mein beßres Ich!

"Dedication," from *Myrtle*

You my soul, you my heart,
You my delight, oh you my pain,
You my world, in which I live,
My heaven you, in which I soar,
Oh you my grave, into which
I eternally pour my sorrow.

You are rest, you are peace,
You are granted to me from heaven.
That you love me makes me worthy,
Your gaze has transfigured my view of myself,
You lift me lovingly above myself,
My good spirit, my better self!

Robert Schumann
Papillons, Op. 2, No. 6

This movement is drawn from a set of twelve short piano works (*Butterflies*), which was published in 1831. During this time, Schumann was coping with degenerative weakness in the middle finger of his right hand, which turned him away from performance and toward literary interests. In some of his writings, he draws links between this composition and a literary inspiration: the final chapters of Jean Paul's *Flegeljahre,* which depict characters at a masked ball.

John Philip Sousa (1854–1932)

"The Stars and Stripes Forever"

Shortly after the American bandleader John Philip Sousa composed "The Stars and Stripes Forever" for his band, the march rapidly became Sousa's most popular work: it was widely distributed in a piano score (below), played at nearly all of his concerts, and later was designated the national march of the United States. A short score excerpt is included to show the piece as a conductor would see it.

Piano score

Short score (excerpt)

John Philip Sousa
"The Washington Post" (piano score)

Sousa wrote this march in 1889, when he was director of the United States Marine Band. The march, which was frequently used for dancing the two-step, was commissioned by the *Washington Post* and first performed at an awards ceremony for the newspaper's essay contest.

Igor Stravinsky (1882–1971)

"Lento," from *For the Five Fingers*

Stravinsky's *For the Five Fingers* is a collection of short teaching pieces composed in 1921. Each movement develops five-note melodies in the right hand, and only occasionally requires a change of right-hand position.

Igor Stravinsky
Danse russe, from *Trois mouvements de Petrouchka*

Stravinsky's *Petrouchka*, originally performed in 1911, is a ballet set at a carnival and tells the story of a puppet that comes to life. The puppet—a stock figure also known as Pulcinella—falls in love with a ballerina but is foiled by her fondness for a handsome Moor. The ballet was the result of Stravinsky's collaboration with the impresario Sergei Diaghilev, whose *Ballets Russes* dancers performed ballets on Russian subjects in Paris. Other collaborations between Stravinsky and Diaghilev included *The Firebird* and *Rite of Spring*.

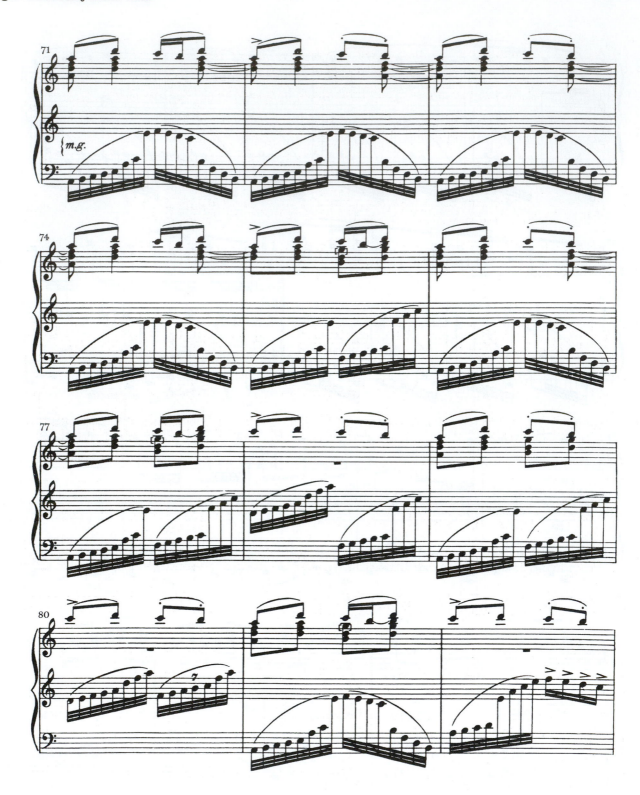

John Tavener (b. 1944)
"The Lamb"

Taverner composed "The Lamb" in 1982 as a birthday gift for his nephew. The text comes from William Blake's 1789 collection of poetry, *Songs of Innocence*. Though Blake set the poem to music himself, his composition has been lost.

Text by William Blake

John Tavener "The Lamb"

Edgard Varèse (1883–1965)

Density 21.5, for solo flute

The French composer Edgard Varèse wrote this piece in 1936 for the flute virtuoso Georges Barrère. The title refers to Barrère's platinum flute: the density of platinum is 21.5 grams per cubic centimeter.

Written in January 1936 at the request of Georges Barrère for the inauguration of his platinum flute. Revised April 1946. 21.5 is the density of platinum.

** Always strictly in time—follow metronomic indications.

*** Notes marked + to be played softly, hitting the keys at the same time to produce a percussive effect.

Anton Webern (1883–1945)

"Dies ist ein Lied," from *Fünf Lieder aus "Der siebente Ring"*

Webern composed this song in 1922 as part of a collection of five songs to texts by the German poet Stefan George. George, whose poems were also set to music by Schoenberg, is considered a pivotal figure in modernist German poetry. The songs are Webern's first works that do not employ key signatures.

Text by Stefan George

TEXT AND TRANSLATION

"Dies ist ein Lied," from *Fünf Lieder aus*
"Dersiebente Ring"

Dies ist ein Lied
Für dich allein:
Von kindischem Wähnen
Von frommen Tränen . . .
Durch Morgengärten klingt es
Ein leichtbeschwingtes.
Nur dir allein
Möcht es ein Lied
Das rühre sein.

"This Is a Song," from *Five Songs from*
"The Seventh Ring"

This is a song
For you alone:
Of childish imagination
Of pious tears . . .
Through the morning garden it sounds
Lightly lilting.
Only for you alone
Would it like to be a song
That stirs the soul.

Anton Webern
String Quartet, Op. 5, third and fourth movements

These are two of five very short movements for string quartet that Webern composed in 1909, and later arranged for string orchestra. They are typical of Webern's works in that they are quite brief; indeed, all of Webern's music (including unpublished works) can be heard in fewer than 8 hours.

Third movement

Fourth movement

Anton Webern
Variations for Piano, Op. 27, second movement

Webern composed this set of variations in 1935–36. In his serial works, Webern frequently made use of older forms, such as theme and variations and binary form. This movement makes unusual use of hand crossing. Try it out by sitting at a keyboard and placing your hands on the pitches designated in the score—but keeping those notated in the upper staff in your right hand, and those in the lower staff in your left.

Hugo Wolf (1860–1903)

"In dem Schatten meiner Locken,"
from *Spanisches Liederbuch*

Wolf published his *Spanisches Liederbuch,* a collection of songs set to German translations of Spanish poetry, in 1891. In the late nineteenth century, Germans were fascinated by what they considered to be the "exoticism" of Spain; consequently, Spanish poetry was popular. The text is a Renaissance poem that was also set by Brahms.

Text by Paul Heyse after Anonymous Spanish text

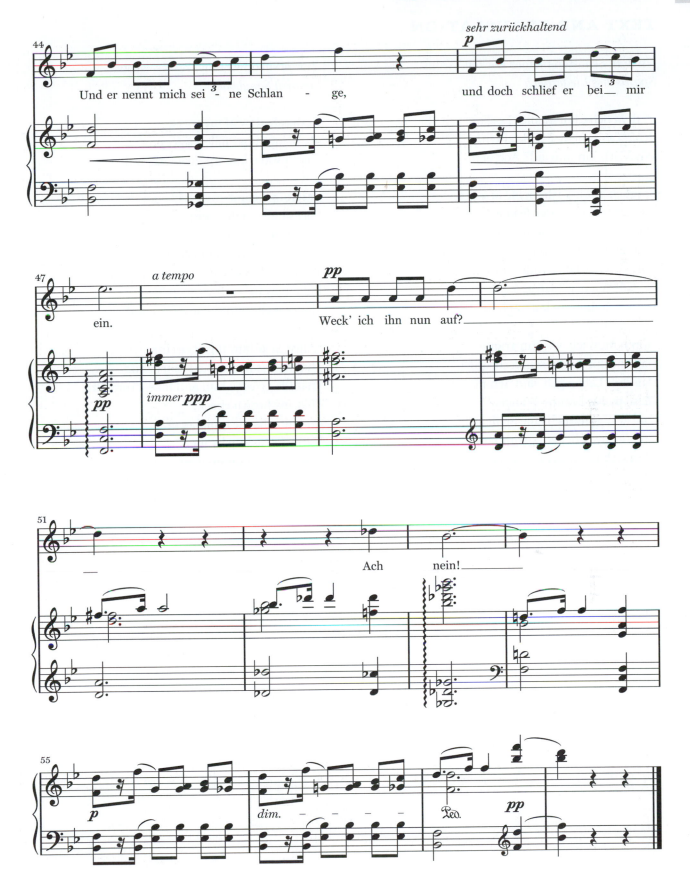

TEXT AND TRANSLATION

"In dem Schatten meiner Locken," from
Spanisches Liederbuch

In dem Schatten meiner Locken
Schlief mir mein Geliebter ein.
Weck' ich ihn nun auf? Ach nein!

Sorglich strählt' ich meine krausen
Locken täglich in der Frühe,
Doch umsonst ist meine Mühe,
weil die Winde sie zersausen.
Lockenschatten, Windessausen
Schläferten den Liebsten ein.
Weck' ich ihn nun auf? Ach nein!

Hören muß ich, wie ihn gräme,
Daß er schmachtet schon so lange,
Daß ihm Leben geb' und nehme
Diese meine braune Wange,
Und er nennt mich eine Schlange,
Und doch schlief er bei mir ein.
Weck' ich ihn nun auf? Ach nein!

"In the shadow of my tresses," from
Spanish Songbook

In the shadow of my tresses
My beloved has fallen asleep.
Shall I wake him up now? Ah, no!

Carefully I comb my curly
Locks daily in the morning,
But in vain is my labor,
Because the winds tousle them.
Tress-shadows, wind-sweeping
Lulled my beloved to sleep.
Shall I wake him up now? Ah, no!

I must hear how it grieves him,
That he has languished for so long,
That life gives to him and takes from him
This, my brown cheek,
And he calls me a snake,
Yet he fell asleep by me.
Shall I wake him up now? Ah, no!

Timeline of Works

Hymn Tunes and Folk Songs

"Chartres" (15th-century French melody, harmonization by Charles Wood)

"Old Hundredth" (harmonization by Louis Bourgeois, 1551)

"Rosa Mystica" (traditional melody, harmonization by Michael Praetorius, 1609)

"St. Anne" (William Croft, 1708)

"America" ("My Country, 'Tis of Thee") (Thesaurus Musicus, 1740)

"The Ash Grove" (Welsh tune, first published 1802)

"St. George's Windsor" (harmonization by George J. Elvey, 1858)

Late 17th Century

Arcangelo Corelli (1653–1713)

Allemanda, from Trio Sonata in A Minor, Op. 4, No. 5 (1694)

Preludio, from Sonata in D Minor, Op. 4, No. 8 (1694)

Henry Purcell (1659–1695)

From *Dido and Aeneas* (1689): "Ah, Belinda, I am prest," "Thy hand, Belinda," and "When I am laid in earth"

"Music for a While" (1692)

Elisabeth-Claude Jacquet de la Guerre (1665–1729)

Gigue, from Suite No. 3 in A Minor (1687)

Early 18th Century

Johann Sebastian Bach (1685–1750)

Passacaglia in C Minor for Organ (1708–1712)

"Soll denn der Pales Opfer" and "Schafe können sicher weiden," from Cantata No. 208 (*The Hunt*) (1713)

Chaconne, from Violin Partita No. 2 in D Minor (1720)

Invention in D Minor (c. 1720)

Invention in F Major (c. 1720)

Minuet I and II, from Cello Suite No. 1 in G Major (c. 1720)

Prelude, from Cello Suite No. 2 in D Minor (c. 1720)

From *The Well-Tempered Clavier*, Book I (1722): Prelude in C Major, Fugue in C Minor, Prelude in C♯ Minor, Fugue in D♯ Minor, and Fugue in G Minor

Chorale, "O Haupt voll Blut und Wunden" (No. 74) (1727)

Chorale, "Aus meines Herzens Grunde" (No. 1) (after 1730)

Chorale, "Ein feste Burg ist unser Gott" (No. 20) (after 1730)

Chorale, "Wachet auf" (No. 179) (1731)

"Er kommt," from Cantata No. 140, "Wachet auf" (1731)

Fugue in E♭ Major for Organ (*St. Anne*) (1739)

Chorale Prelude on "Wachet auf" (Schübler chorale) (1748–1749)

Anonymous

Minuet in D Minor, from the *Anna Magdalena Bach Notebook* (c. 1725)

George Frideric Handel (1685–1759)

Chaconne in G Major (1733)

From *Messiah* (1741): "Rejoice greatly" and "Thy rebuke hath broken His heart"

Late 18th Century

Joseph Haydn (1732–1809)

Concerto in D Major for Corno di caccia and Orchestra, mvt. 1 (1762)

Piano Sonata No. 9 in F Major, mvt. 3 (1766)

Menuetto and Trio, from String Quartet in D Minor, Op. 76, No. 2 (*Quinten*) (1797)

Muzio Clementi (1752–1832)

Sonatina in C Major, Op. 36, No. 1, mvt. 1 (1797)

Sonatina in F Major, Op. 36, No. 4, mvt. 1 (1797)

Wolfgang Amadeus Mozart (1756–1791)

Minuet in F Major, K. 2 (1762)

Minuet, from Sonata for Piano and Violin in C Major, K. 6 (1762–1763)

Piano Sonata in G Major, K. 283, mvt. 1 (1775)

Piano Sonata in D Major, K. 284, mvt. 3 (1775)

Variations on "Ah, vous dirai-je Maman" (1781–1782)

Piano Sonata in F Major, K. 332, mvt. 3 (1783)

String Quartet in D Minor, K. 421, mvt. 1 and mvt. 3 (1783)

From *The Marriage of Figaro* (1786): "Quanto duolmi, Susanna" and "Voi, che sapete"

Piano Sonata in C Major, K. 545 (1788)

From *Requiem* (1791): Kyrie eleison (excerpt) and Dies irae

Ludwig van Beethoven (1770–1827)

Sonatina in F Major, Op. Posth., mvt. 2 (c. 1790–1792)

Piano Sonata in F Minor, Op. 2, No. 1, mvt. 1 (1794–1795)

Piano Sonata in E♭ Major, Op. 7, mvt. 2 (1796)

Piano Sonata in C Minor, Op. 13 (*Pathétique*) (1799)

Piano Sonata in C Major, Op. 53 (*Waldstein*), mvt. 1 (1805)

Für Elise (1810)

Seven Variations on "God Save the King" (1820)

Early 19th Century

Franz Schubert (1797–1828)

"Erlkönig" (1815)

Waltz in B Minor, Op. 18, No. 6 (1815)

"Du bist die Ruh" (1823)

From *Die schöne Müllerin* (1823): "Der Neugierige" and "Morgengruβ"
"Der Lindenbaum," from *Winterreise* (1828)
From *Moments musicaux*, Op. 94: No. 6 in A♭ Major (1828)

Fanny Mendelssohn Hensel (1805–1847)
"Neue Liebe, neues Leben" (1836)
"Nachtwanderer" (published 1848)

Frédéric Chopin (1810–1849)
Nocturne in E♭ Major, Op. 9, No. 2 (1832)
Prelude in C Minor, Op. 28, No. 20 (1839)
Mazurka in F Minor, Op. 68, No. 4 (1846)

Robert Schumann (1810–1856)
Papillons, Op. 2, No. 6 (1831)
From *Dichterliebe* (1840): "Im wunder-schönen Monat Mai" and "Ich grolle nicht"
"Widmung," from *Myrthen* (1840)
From *Album for the Young*, Op. 68 (1848): No. 3: "Trällerliedchen," No. 8: "Wilder Reiter," and No. 9: "Volksliedchen"

Clara Schumann (1819–1896)
"Liebst du um Schönheit" (1841)
Romanze, Op. 21, No. 1 (1853)

Late 19th Century

Stephen Foster (1826–1864)
"Oh! Susanna" (1847)
"Jeanie with the Light Brown Hair" (1854)

Johannes Brahms (1833–1897)
"Die Mainacht" (1866)
Variations on a Theme by Haydn, theme (1873)
Intermezzo in A Major, Op. 118, No. 2 (1893)

Gabriel Fauré (1845–1924)
"Après un rêve" (1877)

John Philip Sousa (1854–1932)
"The Washington Post" (1889)
"The Stars and Stripes Forever" (1897)

Hugo Wolf (1860–1903)
"In dem Schatten meiner Locken," from *Spanisches Liederbuch* (1891)

Early 20th Century

Claude Debussy (1862–1918)
"Fantoches," from *Fêtes galantes* (1891–1892)
"La cathédrale engloutie," from *Préludes*, Book I (1910)

Scott Joplin (c. 1867–1917)
"Pine Apple Rag" (1908)
"Solace" (1909)

Arnold Schoenberg (1874–1951)
Drei Klavierstücke, Op. 11, No. 1 (1909)
Klavierstück, Op. 33a (1929)

Gustav Holst (1874–1934)
Second Suite for Military Band in F Major, mvt. 4, "Fantasia on the 'Dargason'" (1911)

Charles Ives (1874–1954)
"The Cage" (1922)

Maurice Ravel (1875–1937)
Pavane pour une infante défunte (1899)
"Aoua!," from *Chansons madécasses*, for flute, cello, piano, and soprano (1925–1926)

Béla Bartók (1881–1945)
Bagatelle, Op. 6, No. 2 (1908)
"Song of the Harvest," for two violins (1931)
From *Mikrokosmos* (1940): "Bulgarian Rhythm" (No. 115), "From the Isle of Bali" (No. 109), and "Whole-Tone Scale" (No. 136)

Igor Stravinsky (1882–1971)
Danse russe, from *Trois mouvements de Petrouchka* (1910–1911)
"Lento," from *For the Five Fingers* (1921)

Anton Webern (1883–1945)
"Dies ist ein Lied," from *Fünf Lieder aus "Der siebente Ring"* (1909)
String Quartet, Op. 5, mvt. 3 and mvt. 4 (1909)
Variations for Piano, Op. 27, mvt. 2 (1935–1936)

Edgard Varèse (1883–1965)
Density 21.5, for solo flute (1936)

Alban Berg (1885–1935)
"Sahst du nach dem Gewitterregen," from *Fünf Orchester-Lieder* (1912)

Jerome Kern (1885–1945)
"Look for the Silver Lining" (1920)

George Gershwin (1898–1937)
"I Got Rhythm," from *Girl Crazy* (1930)

Late 20th Century

Luigi Dallapiccola (1904–1975)
"Die Sonne kommt!," from *Goethe-lieder*, for voice and clarinets (1953)

Samuel Barber (1910–1981)
"Sea-Snatch," from *Hermit Songs* (1952–1953)

Krzysztof Penderecki (b. 1933)
Threnody for the Victims of Hiroshima (1960)

Steve Reich (b. 1936)
Piano Phase (1967)

John Corigliano (b. 1938)
"Come now, my darling," from *The Ghosts of Versailles* (1987)

John Tavener (b. 1944)
"The Lamb" (1982)

Index of Teaching Points

Credits